Environmental Education

Practice and Possibility

Edited by Ian Robottom

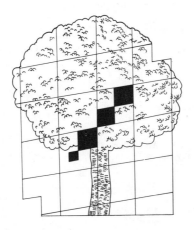

Deakin
University

This book forms part of the ECT317 *Environmental Education* course offered by the School of Education in Deakin University's Open Campus Program. It has been edited by Ian Robottom for the Environmental Education course team, whose members are:

Giovanna Di Chiro
Ian Robottom, Chair
Jim Turner

The following people also wrote for and participated in the planning of the course:

Noel Gough, Victoria College
Annette Greenall, Department of the Arts, Sport, the
    Environment, Tourism and Territories
Robert Stevenson, University of
    Wisconsin — Madison

The course includes:

Deakin University, *Issues in Teaching Environmental Education*
I. Robottom (ed.), *Environmental Education: Practice and Possibility**
*This book is available from Deakin University Press, Deakin University, Victoria 3217

Published by Deakin University, Victoria 3217
Distributed by Deakin University Press
First published 1987

Edited, designed and typeset by
Deakin University Production Unit
Printed by Brown Prior Anderson Pty Ltd, Burwood, Victoria 3125

National Library of Australia
Cataloguing-in-publication data

Environmental education: practice and possibility.

Bibliography.
ISBN 0 7300 0543 7.

1. Environmental education. 2. Education and state. I. Robottom, Ian M. (Ian Morris), 1949–. II. Deakin University. School of Education. Open Campus Program.

333.7'07

Contents

Introduction   1

A political history of environmental
education in Australia: Snakes and ladders
Annette Greenall   3

Environmental education and the question of gender:
A feminist critique
Giovanna Di Chiro   23

Learning with environments: Towards an ecological paradigm
for education
Noel Gough   49

Schooling and environmental education: Contradictions in
purpose and practice
Robert B. Stevenson   69

Towards inquiry-based professional development in
environmental education
Ian Robottom   83

Contributors   121

Acknowledgments   123

Introduction

AS THE TITLE *Environmental Education: Practice and Possibility* suggests, this book describes *practices* in environmental education and points to *possibilities* in the field. The intention is to appraise selected past and current practices in order to prepare the ground for a consideration of alternative images of environmental education that may shape future action.

Annette Greenall's essay, 'A political history of environmental education in Australia: Snakes and ladders', is written from the perspective of a participant in environmental education at the national level. It demonstrates both the influence of party politics on educational innovation and the internally politicised character of national curriculum development in environmental education.

In her essay 'Environmental education and the question of gender: A feminist critique', Giovanna Di Chiro argues that the adoption of a critical feminist perspective of environmental education is an appropriate response to the perceived socio-environmental crisis. The essay identifies sexist interpretations of human–environment relations and contributes to the book's view of the essentially political nature of environmental education.

'Learning with environments: Towards an ecological paradigm for education', by Noel Gough, criticises the dominant paradigm informing environmental education and argues that the epistemological paradigm underlying the whole of education should be replaced by an ecological worldview. Gough's essay shows that environmental education – even education generally – can and should be regarded as problematic at its most fundamental level.

Bob Stevenson's essay, 'Schooling and environmental education: Contradictions in purpose and practice', also treats environmental education as problematic and argues more sharply that there are a number of contradictions between the policy, organisation and practices of conventional schooling, on the one hand, and the socially critical charter of environmental education, on the other.

The final essay, 'Towards inquiry-based professional development in environmental education' by Ian Robottom, analyses the origins, tensions and contradictions in institutional environmental education and concludes that the original cutting edge of environmental educaton has been blunted by the adoption of a technocratic, bureaucratically dominated approach to educational change. The essay suggests that a review of professional development in environmental education is required and advocates an inquiry-based, practitioner research approach.

Overall, the book adopts a political view of environmental education. It sees both environmental issues (where environmental values and actions are in contention) and environmental educational issues (where educational values and actions are in contention) as inherently political. Notwithstanding this common feature, the essays are written from different perspectives and the arguments advanced therein are not all in harmony. To this extent they reflect the contested character of environmental education.

Some of the issues discussed in the book are:

- the essentially social and political character of environmental problems;
- the 'slogan system' of environmental education: exploitation of the generic, ambiguous nature of the term 'environmental education';
- competing self-interests in environmental education policy, organisation and activities;
- the relationship between conventional patterns of schooling and the socially critical aspirations of environmental education;
- the incorporation of environmental education in the existing hegemony of traditional schooling;
- distorted views of the terms 'environment' and 'environmental problem' associated with patriarchal environmental education;
- fundamental inconsistencies between schooling informed by an epistemological paradigm and an ecological paradigm of education; and
- alternative images of professional development in environmental education.

Recognising the political character of environmental education is the first step to developing an argument for a non-technocratic approach to professional development in the field. The book develops this argument by advocating practitioner research in environmental education and concludes with a number of guidelines for inquiry-based professional development.

Ian Robottom
School of Education
Deakin University

A political history of environmental education in Australia: Snakes and ladders

Annette Greenall

... The nation tends to reduce political, social, and economic problems to educational ones and claims to expect schools to cure present ills and provide for a brighter tomorrow for individuals and the collectivity ... (Hazlett 1979, p. 133)

Introduction

POLITICAL PROBLEMS HAVE been intrinsic to the development and practice of environmental education in Australia ever since its formal recognition in 1970. At that time the environment was treated as a politically important issue and environmental education was envisaged as a means for overcoming the 'environmental crisis'. For many, this correlation has continued.

This essay is a critical analysis of the genesis of environmental education as a curriculum issue at national and systemic levels of education from a political perspective and as a working example of participant inquiry. I have participated in the development of environmental education as a national education issue since 1974 through career commitments to the area at the Curriculum Development Centre and the Commonwealth Department of Arts, Heritage and Environment (now the Department of the Arts, Sport, the Environment, Tourism and Territories), and through the Australian Association for Environmental Education. Part of this analysis has already been documented as a case study of national action in environmental education (Greenall 1981).

My perspective throughout the essay is political because of the very nature of the subject matter – environmental education *is a political process*. Using *The Concise Oxford Dictionary* definitions, the perspective will include both the party political – 'of or affecting the State or its government' – and the personal political – 'belonging to or taking a side in politics; relating to a person's or organization's status or influence (a political decision)'. The descriptor 'political' is relevant to the analysis of the emergence of environmental education as an education issue, to the conceptions of environmental education adopted at various times, and to the practice of environmental education in schools.

Beginnings

During the late 1960s and early 1970s the media and popular authors brought the threat of environmental degradation and the nature and implications of the human impact on the environment increasingly to the attention of the general population.[1] The calls for a new ethical principle – concern for the quality of the environment and commitment to the principle of environmental conservation – based on an awareness of the interrelationships between people and their environments also drew attention to the need for education to develop a deeper and more effective environmental consciousness. Ehrlich and Ehrlich, for example, criticised the 'almost total failure [of countries throughout the world] to prepare people to understand and make decisions relating to the population-environment crisis' (Ehrlich & Ehrlich 1972, p. 357).

The term 'environmental education' was first used in an official context in Australia at the 'Education and the Environmental Crisis' national conference, which was convened by the Australian Academy of Science in April 1970. The purposes of the conference were to enquire into the extent to which educational authorities, especially those in Australia, had responded to the perceived environmental crisis by introducing new educational programs and to promote an exchange of views of the responsibilities of educational institutions and the mass media towards the environment (Evans & Boyden 1970).

At this conference O'Neill (1970) reported that environmental education in Australian schools was incidental and totally inadequate. Some conservation education was included in primary school syllabuses and there was some ecological emphasis in biology syllabuses in secondary schools, but in no state was there a specific co-ordinated syllabus which had been designed to increase environmental understanding and motivate students to believe in environmental conservation and restoration. O'Neill believed that there was an urgent need for education authorities to assume a more positive role in response to the environmental crisis.

There were no immediate significant responses to the conference from state education departments or teacher education institutions. During the next few years, however, a number of forces for change in education in Australia were gathered together under the banner of environmental education, and these received increasing attention from Commonwealth and state authorities as well as from community groups.

Towards national action

In Australia, Commonwealth involvement in education generally and in curriculum development projects specifically is a relatively recent phenomenon. The states were solely responsible for education until the early 1960s. Following political and electoral pressure, however, the Commonwealth began to use its financial power and influence to effect changes in education to meet the demands of the electorate, and the Commonwealth Department of Education and Science was established in 1966. The Commonwealth government first became involved in the development of curriculum materials for schools in 1969 when it participated in the funding of the Australian Science Education Project (ASEP).[2] Following its successful involvement in ASEP, the Commonwealth government became involved in other curriculum areas, and ASEP was succeeded in 1974 by the Social Education Materials Project (SEMP), which was co-ordinated by the recently established Curriculum Development Centre (CDC). Such major co-operative projects were seen as enhancing the infant CDC's credibility and giving it a national co-ordinating role.

In the early 1970s, politicians and environmentalists looked more and more to environmental education as a means for addressing and overcoming the environmental crisis. For example, the 1973 Australian Labor Party (ALP) platform on the environment included as an objective: 'Develop and encourage education programs aimed at increasing awareness of, and concern for, the environment' (Australian Labor Party

1973, p. 23).[3] It was to be expected, then, with the election of a Federal Labor Government in December 1972, that environmental education would be one of the five priority areas for curriculum materials development for the CDC upon its interim establishment in 1973. From the beginning, however, environmental education curriculum development by the CDC was subject to political posturing. Educators, especially those in bureaucracies, did not give it the importance its CDC priority status would have suggested. Many academics viewed environmental education as a cultural rather than an educational priority and, according to Spring, the Principal Executive Officer of the CDC Interim Council, several council members regarded it more as a political priority. In their opinion, the curriculum was already overcrowded and environmental education could be accommodated within existing subjects. They also looked on it with a jaundiced eye because, for a variety of reasons, they believed it was associated with the Australian Council for Educational Research and the recently completed ASEP, which was out of favour in their particular states (Greenall 1981).

A first proposal

In October 1974, the CDC Interim Council established an Environmental Education Committee which investigated the requirements for environmental education in Australian schools and prepared a set of recommendations for CDC action. Its interim report, which was circulated at the May 1975 Australian National Commission for the United Nations Educational, Scientific and Cultural Organization (UNESCO) Seminar on Education and the Human Environment (and elsewhere), revealed that by far the most widely perceived need was for teacher education. There was a need to develop teachers' awareness and understanding of environmental education, to change teachers' attitudes towards environmental education, to develop teachers' skills and to increase communication and the exchange of ideas among teachers. The committee accepted teacher education as the primary focal point for CDC involvement, with the ultimate focus being students (Greenall 1981) and proposed an action plan, which is illustrated in Figure 1.

Figure 1

The CDC Environmental Education Committee's action plan for environmental education

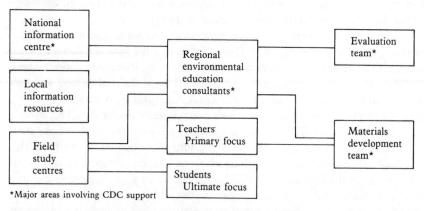

Source: A. Greenall, *Environmental Education in Australia: Phenomenon of the Seventies* (A Case Study in National Curriculum Development), Occasional Paper no. 7, Curriculum Development Centre, Canberra, 1981, p. 145.

The action plan assumed that if teachers were given access to consultants and opportunities to develop their skills, change their attitudes, increase their knowledge and exchange ideas with other teachers, they would help students achieve the aims of environmental education. The CDC would have a co-ordinating role in the action plan as well as contributing to the financing of it.

In many ways the plan proposed a new model of curriculum development in an attempt to meet the needs and characteristics of environmental education. It recognised that materials were not enough: if there was to be an effect in schools a multifaceted, comprehensive program was required. Noting the experience of ASEP, it accepted that direct support for teachers was essential if implementation was to be successful. Although the model was based strongly on the research, development, dissemination and adoption paradigm of educational innovation, there were leanings towards more political and cultural perspectives of innovation: despite the centre–periphery approach, there was some recognition of the value of personal face-to-face interaction (House 1979).

Committee members believed the plan to be ambitious but realistic in the prevailing educational and social climate. No consideration was given to the political implications of its implementation, however. The plan assumed that teachers were simply eagerly awaiting some assistance to implement environmental educational programs. It did not foresee a need to convince teachers in general of the need for environmental education, nor did it anticipate a requirement to explain the implications of a process of education which emphasised attitude and behaviour changes rather than content. Indeed, it did not give much detail of the meaning of environmental education – perhaps as a political expediency. If it had, it may well have received widespread rejection.

Initially the plan did not give the states a large role – it was regionally based, which was consistent with the thinking of the Federal Labor Government. Given the states' rights politics which prevail in Australia, it is realistic to expect that the state education departments would resent their negligible role in the plan, and they did. The revised action plan, which was submitted to the first meeting of the CDC Council in August 1975, gave much greater recognition to state activities and a large funding role to the states, and significantly reduced the emphasis on the CDC's co-ordinating role. Nevertheless, the committee's final report, which included the revised action plan, still recommended a major national environmental education project (Curriculum Development Centre Environmental Education Committee 1975).[4]

In 1975, then, the prospects for the development of a national environmental education project seemed rosy, but the CDC Council then sent the proposal down a snake: while reaffirming environmental education as a priority area, it deferred action. There were several reasons for deferring action, and each reflected the problematic and political nature of the development of environmental education in Australia.

The 1975 Federal budget, which was to have been expansionist for the CDC, instead cut CDC funds, and all new developments, including environmental education, were deferred. In addition, the Australian Education Council representatives on the CDC Council considered the proposal too ambitious. Some council members continued to associate environmental education with ASEP and, because they were now disenchanted with both ASEP and SEMP, they reacted against another large comprehensive curriculum project. Moreover, this proposal was so expensive (costing approximately two million dollars over three years) that it would have shut out other curriculum projects, even if the CDC had had the funds for this one. Finally, the proposal would have overwhelmed the states' funds, even if they had been supportive.

At the end of 1975, then, the CDC still considered environmental education a priority area, but no project had been funded. Broad political support for environmental education, and for the environment generally, was also waning (down another snake?) with the removal from office of the Labor Government.

A second attempt

The prospects for national action on environmental education went up a ladder in late 1976 with the establishment of a CDC Study Group on Environmental Education. The group's brief was to make recommendations on curriculum programs in which the CDC could co-operate with the states and which would assist school-based curriculum development. There had been a definite swing away from a centre–periphery approach to educational innovation towards a political-cultural approach, focusing on school-based curriculum development.

The study group made recommendations in five areas which it saw as sequential: developing general acceptance of environmental education, providing support for diffusion and teacher awareness, developing materials, expanding the CDC information service, and facilitating the formation of a National Environmental Education Council (Curriculum Development Centre Study Group on Environmental Education 1977). These recommendations were the foundation of the CDC environmental education program from 1977 to 1980.

There was a paradox in the study group's report. It seemed to recognise that activities conducted in formal education settings in the name of environmental education did not necessarily meet the group's perceptions of environmental education. Environmental education was perceived to be 'in a state of emergence within the educational curriculum, rather than being an established component of it' (Curriculum Development Centre Study Group on Environmental Education 1977, p. 17), but, instead of recommending the development of new materials which would exemplify the emerging nature of environmental education, the report suggested that case studies of existing practices be produced. This appears to have been a misplaced adherence to a belief in a cultural context for innovation, and it led to difficulties in the project which was eventually developed from the recommendations.

There was one significant advance. The study group did not believe, as the 1974 committee appeared to, that teachers were eagerly awaiting assistance to become involved in environmental education, so its first priority was to increase teacher awareness of the status and multifaceted nature of environmental education. But political expediencies intruded into the study group's report, and again no details of the aims or definitions of environmental education and no specific guidelines on assistance for teachers were provided. This aspect is discussed later in this essay.

Despite the study group's urging that the sequence of its recommendations be maintained, the strongest support from state education departments and other bodies was for teacher education: the production of case studies, papers and evaluation reports for teachers, and in-service activities. Publicity materials aimed at increasing awareness were given a low priority. Given the strong support for teachers' materials, it was to be expected that the development of these would be the focus of the Environmental Education Project finally approved by the CDC Council in February 1978 (Greenall 1981).

This project was decentralised in its structure and relied on co-operation with the states. It aimed to provide non-prescriptive materials to assist teachers in their class-room practices and offered small grants to teachers to describe their existing programs or their position on a particular topic related to environmental education. The call for submissions did not define environmental education, although it did specify that the projects had to be clearly identified as being within the area of environmental edu-cation. The submissions that were received met neither the expectations nor the pri-orities of the project. They revealed that much that was believed to be environmental education, or was put forward as such, was mainly nature study and outdoor education. It was expected that the project would encourage education *for* the environment, but very few of the submissions incorporated affective or action-oriented objectives. Rather, the submissions were characterised by the cognitive objectives of education *about* the environment. Interdisciplinary environmental education was also a high priority of the project, yet few submissions involved more than one or two traditional disciplines. A similar phenomenon has been noted in geography-based environmental programs in the United Kingdom (Huckle 1983) and by Lucas (1980), who remarked on the preponderance of *in* the environment and *about* the environment programs, many of which are science based, posing as environmental education in schools. The project attempted to overcome deficiencies in the submissions by commissioning papers for inclusion in its publications. For example, to illustrate how environmental education could be implemented in a secondary school, a paper was commissioned on 'Developing a school policy on environmental education', and to demonstrate how environmental education could relate to a subject other than science or geography, there was a paper on 'Environmental education and the home economics teacher'. The materials were published as two sourcebooks, one for primary education and one for secondary edu-cation. There were also three publications suitable for the upper primary/lower secon-dary level—a simulation game, a book of outdoor activities and a book about urban environment activities (Environmental Education Project 1980–81).

In spite of these shortcomings, the project did develop a successful liaison officer network—consisting of eight nominated state and Territory education department liaison officers—for the exchange of information and ideas and for a certain degree of co-ordination. This network fostered the formation of the Australian Association for Environmental Education as a means for continuing communication between those interested in environmental education.

Between 1977 and 1980 the CDC established two other projects as part of its environmental education program. Both received most of their funding from agencies other than the CDC and were more centralised in their development. One, Environ-mental Education for Schools, was funded by the Commonwealth Department of Environment, Housing and Community Development to produce publicity materials to promote environmental education in schools. These materials became a general policy guidelines statement which was distributed to all schools in 1980 (Greenall 1980). The statement presented environmental education as an orientation in the curriculum and gave details of the objectives and strategies for implementing environmental education in schools.

The second project was a joint one with the Australian Heritage Commission (Cur-riculum Development Centre 1980). This was an experiment in a new style of curric-ulum development which involved both teachers and people outside formal education in the development of materials. Although their development was centralised, the materials were intended to be locally adapted and modified, and the aim was to stimulate a culture of innovation by disseminating information about Australia's heritage and strategies for teaching about it. The materials were an interesting mixture of passive knowledge transmission and encouragement to become involved in heritage conservation. They were an attempt at an interdisciplinary project within the realities and restrictions of existing secondary school structures and contained separate units for art, history and science/geography, together with a multidisciplinary unit which could probably best be used by a social studies teacher. The viability of this type of approach to the implementation of environmental education in schools is discussed later in this essay.

The momentum fades

Although there was a semblance of a support network for the dissemination and implementation of environmental education in schools through the liaison officer network of the Environmental Education Project, the reality was quite different in most instances. The network was in place only from 1978 to 1979, but the first published materials did not appear until late 1980. Once again the development but not the dissemination phase of a curriculum project was supported, in spite of past experience showing that without effiicient dissemination the innovation would be less successful. In addition, although the states had agreed that the nominated liaison officers would be released from their other duties for the equivalent of one day a week to participate in the project, in reality the project work was merely added to their other duties and already overstretched commitments.

Yet again the development of environmental education was both problematic and political: that there was a project sent its development up a ladder, but the lack of support brought it down another snake. Even if the liaison officers had wanted to support classroom implementation of the project materials, they did not have the support of their systems to do so, either in terms of time or assistance through the provision of in-service education activity funding.

Also, for political reasons the CDC was able to do little to overcome the difficulties which it knew had haunted the implementation of both ASEP and SEMP: once the materials were published there was little support for their dissemination and implementation. In-service education funds had certainly increased since the early 1970s, but the Schools Commission and the states were unwilling to allocate resources to dissemination of CDC project materials. Because of the way in which the in-service education system had been established, the CDC had great difficulty in nominating and receiving funding for dissemination activities, and with the liasion officer network dismantled before the materials were available there was little incentive for people in the states to nominate the project materials for in-service education funds.

A related action which may well have influenced the lack of support for dissemination of the project materials in the states was the winding down of the CDC's own activities in environmental education in 1980. The Director and Council believed that sufficient resources had been devoted to environmental education and that other competing areas were growing in importance. From 1980 onwards, CDC activities in environmental education were directed at distribution of the published materials rather than at attempts to change people and processes in favour of environmental education (Greenall 1980).

At this time there was a possibility that environmental studies would be included in the CDC's proposal for a core curriculum for Australian schools (Curriculum Development Centre 1980a)—the plan was that environmentalism would permeate the core, a notion which was consistent with the CDC policy statement on environmental education (Greenall 1980). But the CDC was abolished (another political act) in April 1981 before the core curriculum statement could be much expanded, so it is difficult to predict how the relationship between environmental education and the core curriculum would have been pursued at the national level. Discussion later in this essay will analyse how some states took up this challenge.

A new beginning?

Two significant national events in 1983 raised expectations that environmental education would again become a priority for action at the national level. The first was the election of the Hawke Labor Government: since the ALP platform still included a policy on environmental education, perhaps a Labor Government would make environmental education a priority again. The second was the production of *A National Conservation Strategy for Australia (NCSA)* (Department of Home Affairs and Environment 1984), based on the *World Conservation Strategy* which had been launched by the International Union for the Conservation of Nature and Natural Resources (IUCN) in 1980 (IUCN 1980).

The *NCSA* is a potentially significant document. Within an overall philosophy of 'living resource conservation for sustainable development', it states that education and training are one of the areas for priority national action for achieving this goal. The *NCSA* has been endorsed by the Commonwealth and most state and Territory governments. Some states are also developing their own conservation strategies, all of which give prominence to the role of education in achieving the goal of sustainable development. The *NCSA* challenges the Australian community to redress the errors of the past and to keep options open in order to optimise the quality of life for all Australians. The basic premise is that there is a need for people to hold values which will sustain society rather than destroy it. In the words of the Prime Minister in the Foreword to the *NCSA*:

> Unless we conserve [our renewable resources] for sustainable development it will be our children and their children who will pay the price of our neglect. (Department of Home Affairs and Environment 1984, p. 3)

Thus the need for social reconstruction is being accepted, and education has a key role to play in it. Indeed, in many ways the *NCSA* provides a basis for a role for environmental education that was only dreamed about in the early 1970s.

Although the importance of the environment as an electoral issue is no longer underestimated, the environment and environmental education are still not seen as dominant political priority areas by the major parties. Environmental education continues to be given a low priority by bureaucrats within both environment and education ministries. There is an environmental education unit within the Commonwealth Department of the Arts, Sport, the Environment, Tourism and Territories, but it has been downgraded since its establishment as the Department of Arts, Heritage and Environmment in 1983 and now has fewer staff and resources to promote the implementation of the *NCSA* and environmental awareness and participation in environmental decision making by the community. Similar cuts have affected the equivalent units in the various state environment agencies.

The CDC was reconstituted as part of the Schools Commission when the Federal Labor Government was elected in 1983. In spite of the ALP policy to re-establish 'the environment [sic] education function in the Curriculum Development Centre' (Australian Labor Party 1982) and the importance given to education in the NCSA, the Schools Commission and the Minister for Education have not made environmental education a priority area. There are many competing curriculum interests, and many believe that enough has been done for environmental education. However, a paper entitled 'Living in Harmony with the Australian Environment' was commissioned as part of the Bicentennial Australian Studies Schools Project of the Schools Commission, and this is to be distributed to all schools in 1987 (Fien, in press). At this stage this would seem to be the most that can be expected from the Commonwealth education ministry.

The allusion to snakes and ladders continues. The encouraging ladders of the election of a Labor government and the endorsement of the NCSA have been more than matched by the discouraging snakes of the economic and political situation which gives areas other than the environment and environmental education higher priority.

Environmental education and the states

It has already been noted that, from the early 1970s, the state education departments did not give environmental education a high priority, although this did not stop them implementing some environmental education activities. Environmental education was interpreted as education *in* the environment and education *about* the environment, however, and the states' syllabus statements at both primary and secondary levels reflected this interpretation (Linke 1977). In the mid-1970s, very few of these activities had attitudinal or action components, 'education *for* the environment'. By 1977 three states had produced policy statements on environmental education, and since then the other three have recognised its place in the curriculum. None gives it particularly high priority, and few provide much support in the form of resources.

The Western Australian Director-General of Education released a policy statement in 1977 which reiterated the 1975 Belgrade Charter but provided little support for teachers to implement it (Western Australian Department of Education 1977). This statement still stands. The Tasmanian Education Department released a statement in 1976 which seemed to be directed at secondary science teachers and gave the ASEP objectives prominence (Tasmanian Education Department 1976). The 1977 Queensland Department of Education statement gave guidelines to schools and described the support services available for teachers (Queensland Department of Education 1976). Both attitudinal and action components were included in its description of environmental education. A revised statement for distribution to schools in 1987 is planned.

In 1981 the South Australian Education Department included environmental education as one of the eight recommended areas of a core curriculum (Education Department of South Australia 1981). Here environmental education is to 'provide opportunities for students to develop positive and responsible attitudes towards conserving the natural environment and its resources'. The social environment and social action are overlooked.

While the 1985 Victorian Education Department document on curriculum frameworks omitted environmental education as a distinct entity, it allowed for it to be developed as an orientation in the curriculum, particularly though social education (Education Department of Victoria 1985). A policy statement on environmental education has never been released in Victoria, but there is an environmental education curriculum committee in the Ministry of Education which provides advice on environmental education. The emphasis in Victoria has been mainly to support education *in* the environment and education *about* the environment through education extension and other services, although there has been support from a number of areas for a greater focus on the attitudinal and action components of environmental education programs.

The New South Wales Department of Education plans to release a policy statement with supporting documents on environmental education for schools in 1987. It is likely that these will support the attitudinal and action components of environmental education.

In all these statements the emphasis is still on increasing awareness and knowledge of the (mainly natural) environment and on developing the skills to investigate it, as distinct from the more characteristic aims of environmental education which are concerned with values, attitudes and social action to resolve environmental problems. The statements also neglect the environment in its social context, which should and does affect environmental decision making. Environmental education is primarily about changing people's attitudes and behaviours towards the environment, yet the education authorities continue to downplay these aspects. I have argued elsewhere that environmental education has been subjected to incorporation within the existing hegemony of the epistemological paradigm of traditional education in a neutralised form: the name, and the 'acceptable' knowledge and skills components, have been retained, while the 'radical' action components have been deleted or diluted (Greenall 1981). I believe that this still is the case.

Creating Utopias

Environmental education is political, both as an educational process and as a social force. It is concerned with developing a curriculum which is both socially critical and relevant. It aims to create possible worlds, or achievable Utopias, which are a real improvement on the actual world we inhabit today. Creating such Utopias raises practical questions about 'acting wisely, truly and rightly in the social and political situations in which we find ourselves'. Kemmis (1986 p. 11) has used these words to describe a socially critical curriculum which he and others (Kemmis, Cole & Suggett 1983) have suggested is needed by schools in the late twentieth century. The words are equally applicable to environmental education, for it too is concerned with developing a curriculum which encourages the practice of just, participatory and collaborative decision making and involves critical analysis of the development of the nature, forms and formative processes of society generally and of the power relationships within a particular society. Environmental education is about revealing how the world works and how it might be changed:

> It is about critically examining the economic and political processes shaping the social use of nature within different, but inter-related societies and helping pupils recognize the struggles of those working for greater democracy and an improved environment. (Huckle 1986b, p. 12)

The practice of environmental education in Australian schools has not been consistent with this description. Lessons have tended to stress ecological processes, wilderness areas and the survival needs of rare species and habitats. There has been a reluctance to recognise that environments are socially constructed and that the environmental problems facing the majority of the world's people are problems of hunger, clean water, safe and satisfying work, housing and alienation (Huckle 1986b).

Lessons about ecological processes and the like are politically safe (and easier to teach), and, because they can be said to be increasing environmental awareness and understanding, some teachers believe that they can call these programs environmental education. But such teaching masks the true causes of environmental problems, excludes radical social alternatives and sustains a technocratic environmentalism which can ameliorate but not solve environmental issues. It is much more concerned with social reproduction than social reconstruction, and a majority of teachers and bureaucrats are more secure with the former. It has been much simpler to incorporate environmental experiences and environmental content into existing school programs and to call them environmental education than to totally re-think the currriculum and adopt a different, say interdisciplinary, approach.

The practice of environmental education, as it should be practised if its aims are to be achieved, means that social reproduction should be challenged by developing students' social and political literacy and by providing students with opportunities for effective participation in relevant real issues. Such practice is consistent with an ecological paradigm for education rather than the existing epistemological one.[5] However, many find such practices threatening. As McElroy has noted in regard to political literacy education:

> It is ironical that the very success of political literacy education is what draws the most opposition. Politically literate students are seen as a threat to the established order of power and control. Hence potentially successful political action may be vigorously resisted while ineffective participation . . . is lauded. (McElroy 1986, p. 106)

The same could be said about environmental education programs; if properly implemented, they could be most threatening. Schools therefore resist their implementation and are an impediment to social change.

Changing conceptions of environmental education

Environmental education, as defined by various international bodies and conferences, is concerned with changing individuals and society through existing disciplines and structures. This does not mean that existing disciplines and structures will remain static; rather, the whole school currriculum and organisation will need to change, but still remain within the parameters of existing structures.

These definitions also acknowledge that the traditional formulations of the disciplines are individually inadequate for achieving the aims of environmental education, and they recommend an interdisciplinary approach, not a new or separate subject.

> The field under discussion is vast and multifaceted; it should be approached with a holistic attitude in that man and the innumerable components of his physical and cultural environment should be examined together in order to identify the complex and often hidden interactions which determine the pattern of human concerns. (Buzzati-Traverso 1977, p. 13)

In the early 1970s the most widely accepted definition of environmental education was that proposed by the IUCN:

> Environmental education is the process of recognizing values and clarifying concepts in order to develop skills and attitudes necessary to understand and appreciate the inter-relatedness among man, his culture and his biophysical surroundings. Environmental education also entails practice in decision-making and self-formulation of a code of behaviour about issues concerning environmental quality. (IUCN 1970)

This definition does not provide a workable statement on environmental education, but at the time no concern was expressed about this inadequacy; the arguments were more concerned with the nature of environmental education. In the report of the 1975 UNESCO seminar in Australia Linke recognised this difficulty when he warned that until environmental education 'is defined in a practical way which is accepted by teachers and those who administer education it cannot command a place in the formal curriculum', and therefore 'can have no continuing academic identity' (Linke 1977, p. 12).

In the mid-1970s in Australia, particularly in the preparation of the CDC action plan, there was an attempt to articulate a complete statement on environmental education, but, because those involved found it difficult to find a common ground beyond a general agreement, the formulations simply provided guidelines and assumed that the details would come later. It was also felt that the formulations *should* be general: if they were too specific they may have been rejected. At the time, supporters of environmental education appeared to adopt an ahistorical political perspective of curriculum innovation and to push for a reconceptualised (social reconstructionist) curriculum, given that there was a federal government with reformist philosophies. But there were conflicting expectations of curriculum reform – some saw environmental education as the common culture in schools, whereas others saw it as being incorporated into the existing curriculum based on traditional disciplines (Greenall 1981). These conflicts, which have never really been resolved in schools, confirm the problematic nature of environmental education.

A similar reluctance to provide workable statements for a potentially controversial area was noted by Apple in regard to the progressive education movement in America earlier this century: supporters were 'cautious about even raising the question of what actual content should be taught and evaluated in schools', preferring to concern themselves with teaching methods because 'the determination of curriculum was perceived as inherently a political issue which could split the movement' (Apple 1978, p. 370).

Notwithstanding this lack of definition and systemic support, 'environmental' became the catchcry adjective of the early and mid-1970s, although much of what was put forward as 'environmental education' at this time would not be recognised as such by the criteria accepted later in the decade. Many of the moves towards the environment owed more to attempts to make education 'relevant' than to the aims of environmental education, though many too grew out of concern for the environmental crisis.

The courses, programs and activities which did develop in schools under the banner 'environmental . . .' were frequently an extension of conservation education, as was noted by O'Neill (1970) at the Australian Academy of Science Conference, or an increase in the amount and type of 'nature study', i.e. there was an increasing emphasis on education *about* the environment. There was also an increase in the number of field study centres operated by the state education authorities, i.e. there was an increasing emphasis on education *in* the environment. The emphasis was on the biophysical ('nature') rather than the cultural surroundings, and those surroundings were invariably at a distance from the school: local studies and urban studies were rarely a part of the practice of environmental education. The aim was to increase awareness and understanding of ecological processes and, sometimes, the human impact on these. The intent was passive transmission rather than social action, i.e. there was little education *for* the environment.

It was evident in the preparation of the 1975 CDC action plan that, although there was widespread support for increasing understanding of the environment, those involved with schools were reluctant to provide experiences for students which encouraged clarification of values and participation in decision making. It was felt that such experiences were more appropriate for adults and that schools should confine themselves to increasing students' knowledge of the environment. There was also a belief that if students knew about an issue they might start to be concerned about it and then do something about it. This sequence of behaviours was implicit in the ordering of the aims of environmental education espoused in the documents from the UNESCO United Nations Environmental Programme and, eventually, from the CDC, and explicit in the thinking of science teachers particularly (see Figure 2).

Figure 2
Aims of environmental education

The aims of environmental education are:

- to help students acquire an *awareness* of and *sensitivity* to the total environment
- to help students develop a basic *understanding* of the total environment and the interrelationships of man and the environment
- to help students develop the *skills* necessary for investigating the total environment and for identifying and solving environmental problems
- to help students acquire social values and strong *feelings of concern* for the environment
- to help students acquire the *motivation for actively participating* in environmental improvement and protection
- to help students *identify alternative approaches* and *make informed decisions* about the environment based on ecological, political, economic, social and aesthetic factors
- to provide students with *opportunities to be actively involved* at all levels in working towards the resolution of environmental problems.

Source: A. Greenall, *Environmental Education for Schools*, Curriculum Development Centre, Canberra, 1980, p. 4.

At this time, despite all the statements which stressed its interdisciplinary nature, environmental education was still very much 'owned' by and associated with science teaching. Consequently, the need to have awareness experiences before being able to participate was a common belief. Fensham (in press) recently said that he now believes the reverse to be true: students develop an interest in increasing their awareness and knowledge by being involved in an issue and caring about what happens.

Support for the notion that student experiences should focus on awareness and understanding of the environment rather than participation in the resolution of environmental problems came from both the schools and the state education authorities. The aims of environmental education in the CDC policy statement (see Figure 2) were a compromise based on the statements in the 1975 Belgrade Charter and modified after discussions with state education authorities. Several of the references to environmental problems in the Belgrade Charter were deleted, and the overall emphasis on problems was watered down, because some states felt that statements about environmental education should be positive rather than negative, and an emphasis on environmental problems was seen as a negative approach. Because the CDC wanted to distribute copies of its statement on environmental education to all schools in Australia, a political compromise was reached and the changes were made.

As noted earlier, the submissions received by the CDC Environmental Education Project revealed that environmental education was still in a state of emergence in the curriculum and that much of what was submitted to the project was concerned with increasing knowledge, not encouraging social action. If these submissions were a true reflection of what was happening in schools, and the project's liaison officers believed this to be the case, the lack of workable statements and systemic support had significantly contributed to the problematic nature of the practice of environmental education in Australian schools. Because, for political reasons, no one was willing to say that these practices were not environmental education, the misconceptions were perpetuated.

There were several reasons for not correcting these errors. Although many submissions to the project were rejected because they did not focus upon any of the aims of environmental education (yet their proposers considered that they did, which was a matter for concern), others were accepted for various political reasons. These included a desire to have all states represented, a desire to mask the failure of the project to acknowledge its error in assuming that good practices were already in existence in schools, and a desire to have a tangible product. Some members of the project management committee were concerned that what would emerge as the publications purporting to exemplify good practices (mainly the commissioned papers) would also contain examples which would only reinforce misconceptions about environmental education (e.g. activities designed to increase awareness but not action). There was a need for the project to have products and publications—for political reasons something was better than nothing—so a selection of the project's submissions was published, despite these misgivings.

There were three main obstacles to the formulation of a clear definition of environmental education: firstly, those involved naively assumed that, because 'environmental education' had been around for several years, there was a general understanding of its meaning; secondly, there was a reluctance to define it in case it was rejected; and thirdly, and perhaps most importantly, there was an awareness that the meaning of environmental education was still evolving, so its interpretation could remain fluid if it was not given a precise definition.

Towards a dynamic green future

Environmental education was, and still is, in a dynamic state. Over the past decade and more, the accepted beliefs and many practices have changed from being concerned with education *about* the environment or *in* the environment to education *for* the environment.

Other changes have included growing acceptance of the viability of a separate subject (environmental studies) in some circumstances. While the necessity of an interdisciplinary or holistic approach to environmental education is still recognised, it has become increasingly apparent that this approach is not realistic within the existing structure of most schools, whereas a new subject may be. Experiences with interdisciplinary kits such as *Investigating the National Estate* (Curriculum Development Centre 1980b) showed that individual units were adopted by their traditional discipline area without recognition of the implicit interdisciplinary approach of the whole kit. While there always has been systemic resistance to a separate subject from Western Australia, all other states except Queensland (where the geography syllabus has a strong environmental component) now offer an environmental studies subject at the senior secondary level.

The rhetoric about environmental education has changed as well. In contrast to the general nature of the 1970 IUCN definition of environmental education, the 1980 IUCN *World Conservation Strategy* was more specific:

> Ultimately the behaviour of entire societies towards the biosphere must be transformed if the achievement of conservation objectives is to be assured. A new ethic, embracing plants and animals as well as people, is required for human societies to live in harmony with the natural world on which they depend for survival and wellbeing. The long term task of environmental education is to foster or reinforce attitudes and behaviour compatible with this new ethic. (IUCN 1980, section 13)

The recognition of the role of education in achieving the *NCSA* objectives for 'living resource conservation for sustainable development' has already been noted. These statements provide good political support for environmental education.

Documents such as the *World Conservation Strategy*, although it fails to recognise and challenge the structural obstacles to eco-development (Huckle 1986a), and the writings of people such as Roszak (1980) and Capra (1982) have placed the resolution of environmental problems in the context of the whole social situation and have highlighted once more the need for a social reconstructionist curriculum. For example, Roszak observed that:

> . . . the environmental anguish of the Earth has entered our lives as a radical transformation of human identity. The needs of the planet and the needs of the person have become one, and together they have begun to act upon the central institutions of our society with a force that is profoundly subversive, but which carries within it the promise of cultural renewal. (Roszak 1978, p.xix)

Such statements reinforce the political nature of environmental education. The association of the environment movement with others such as peace, women and labour in Green politics means that the critical anlaysis of the framework of society which is being encouraged through the socially critical curriculum is equally applicable to environmental education. Again there is encouragement to question and participate in resolving environmental problems, but this time it is very much within a political context. Coincidentally, there is a movement for an ecological paradigm in education which is compatible with the political context. The forces for change in education are once again gathering, and environmental education is once more part of them.

The transition to a just and ecologically sustainable society requires an understanding of the environment, society and politics. The conception of environmental education continues to change, and the ladders of the game are once again beckoning. The next throw will reveal whether these new Green political associates of environmental education will take it up a ladder or down yet another snake.

Notes

1 See, for example, Carson (1962), Ehrlich & Ehrlich (1972) and Marshall (1968).
2 ASEP was the first co-operative curriculum development project between the Commonwealth and all the states.
3 Similar statements have continued to be a part of the ALP platform (Greenall 1985).
4 The report was published as a discussion document without financial details (Greenall & Womersley 1977).
5 See Noel Gough's essay in this book.

References

Apple, M. W. (1978), 'Ideology, reproduction, and educational reform', *Comparative Education Review* **22**(3), 367–87.

Australian Labor Party (1973), *Platform, Consititution and Rules* (as approved by the 30th Federal Conference, Surfers Paradise), ALP Federal Secretariat, Canberra.

Australian Labor Party (1982), *Platform, Constitution and Rules* (as approved by the 35th National Conference, Canberra), ALP National Secretariat, Canberra.

Buzzati-Traverso, A. (1977), 'Some thoughts on the philosophy of environmental education', in United Nations Educational, Scientific and Cultural Organization, *Trends in Environmental Education*, UNESCO, Paris.

Capra, F. (1982), *The Turning Point: Society and the Rising Culture*, Simon & Schuster, New York.

Carson, R. (1962), *Silent Spring*, Houghton Mifflin, Boston, Mass.

Curriculum Development Centre (1980a), *Core Curriculum for Australian Schools*, CDC, Canberra.

Curriculum Development Centre (1980b), *Investigating the National Estate*, CDC, Canberra.

Curriculum Development Centre Environmental Education Committee (1975), *A Proposal for the Support of Environmental Education in Australia (Final Report)*, CDC, Canberra (unpublished).

Curriculum Development Centre Study Group on Environmental Education (1977), *Report of the Curriculum Development Centre Study Group on Environmental Education*, Curriculum Development Centre, Canberra.

Department of Home Affairs and Environment (1984), *A National Conservation Strategy for Australia*, AGPS, Canberra.

Education Department of South Australia (1981), *Our Schools and Their Purposes: Into the 80s*, Education Department of South Australia, Adelaide.

Education Department of Victoria (1985), *Curriculum Frameworks P–12: An Introduction*, Education Department of Victoria, Melbourne.

Ehrlich, P. R., & Ehrlich, A. H. (1972), *Population/Resources/Environment: Issues in Human Ecology*, 2nd edn, Freeman, San Francisco.

Environmental Education Project (1980–1981), *Environmental Education: A Sourcebook for Primary Education, Environmental Education: A Sourcebook for Secondary Education, Exploring Outdoors, Streets, Walmit Divided*, Curriculum Development Centre, Canberra.

Evans, J., & Boyden, S. (eds) (1970), *Education and the Environmental Crisis*, Academy Report no. 13, Australian Academy of Science, Canberra.

Fensham, P. J. (in press), 'Environmental education – A Tbilisi benchmark', in Department of Arts, Heritage and Environment, *Environmental Education – Past,*

Present and Future (Proceedings of the Third National Environmental Education Seminar), AGPS, Canberra.

Fien, J. (in press), Living in Harmony with the Environment: An Australian Studies Perspective on Environmental Education, Schools Commission, Canberra (to be published as a Bulletin of the Bicentennial Australian Studies Schools Project).

Greenall, A. (1980), *Environmental Education for Schools*, Curriculum Development Centre, Canberra.

Greenall, A. (1981), *Environmental Education in Australia: Phenomenon of the Seventies* (A Case Study in National Curriculum Development), Occasional Paper no. 7, Curriculum Development Centre, Canberra.

Greenall, A. (1985), 'A new beginning for environmental education in Australia', *Australian Journal of Environmental Education* **1**(2), 13–15.

Greenall, A., & Womersley, J. C. (eds) (1977), *Development of Environmental Education in Australia–Key Issues*, Curriculum Development Centre, Canberra.

Hazlett, J. S. (1979), 'Conceptions of curriculum history', *Curriculum Inquiry* **9**(2), 129–35.

House, E. R. (1979), 'Technology versus craft: A ten year perspective on innovation', *Journal of Curriculum Studies* **11**(1), 1–15.

Huckle, J. (1983), 'Environmental education', in J. Huckle (ed.), *Geographical Education: Reflection and Action*, Oxford University Press, Oxford.

Huckle, J. (1986a), 'Ecological crisis: Some implications for geographical education', *Contemporary Issues in Geographical Education* **2**(2), 2–13.

Huckle, J. (1986b) 'Ten red questions to ask green teachers', *Green Teacher* **1**(2), 11–15.

International Union for the Conservation of Nature and Natural Resources (1980), *World Conservation Strategy: Living Resource Conservation for Sustainable Development*, IUCN, np.

International Union for the Conservation of Nature and Natural Resources Commission on Education (1970), *International Working Meeting on Environmental Education in the School Curriculum*, UNESCO, Paris.

Kemmis, S. (1986), 'Mapping Utopia: Towards a socially critical curriculum', *Interaction* **14**(5), 11–30.

Kemmis, S., Cole, P., & Suggett, D. (1983), *Orientations to Curriculum and Transition: Towards the Socially Critical School*, Victorian Institute for Secondary Education, Melbourne.

Linke, R. D. (1977), 'Environmental education in Australian public schools: A summary of state education department position papers', in R. D. Linke (ed.), *Education and the Human Environment*, Curriculum Development Centre, Canberra.

Lucas, A. M. (1980), 'Science and environmental education: Pious hopes, self praise and disciplinary chauvinism', *Studies in Science Education* **7**, 1–26.

Marshall, A. J. (1968), *The Great Extermination: A Guide to Anglo:Australian Cupidity*, Panther, London.

McElroy, B. (1986), 'Geography's contribution to political literacy' , in J. Fien & R. Gerber (eds), *Teaching Geography for a Better World*, Australian Geography Teachers Association with Jacaranda Press, Brisbane.

O'Neill, B. (1970), 'Environmental education in Australian schools', in J. Evans & S. Boyden (eds), *Education and the Environmental Crisis*, Academy Report no. 13, Australian Academy of Science, Canberra.

Queensland Department of Education (1977), *Environmental Education in Queensland Schools*, Queeensland Department of Education, Brisbane.

Roszak, T. (1978), *Person/Planet: The Creative Disintegration of Industrial Society*, Anchor/Doubleday, New York.

Tasmanian Education Department (1976) *Environmental Education,* Tasmanian Education Department, Hobart.

Western Australian Department of Education (1977), *Environmental Education,* Policy from the Director-General's Office no. 8, Western Australian Department of Education, Perth.

Annotated bibliography

Fien, J., & Gerber, R. (eds). *Teaching Geography for a Better World.* Australian Geography Teachers Association with Jacaranda Press, Brisbane, 1986.

Since the inception of environmental education, no one discipline has been considered capable of catering for it. Terms such as multidisciplinary, interdisciplinary and transdisciplinary have been used to characterise environmental education programs. More than a decade on, however, the implications of these terms for school programs is still being discussed. If any one existing discipline is able to meet the criteria for developing an acceptable environmental education program, it is geography, or at least geography as it is portrayed in *Teaching Geography for a Better World.* This volume contains the major papers from the 1986 Australian Geography Teachers Association national conference. Several of the papers explore issues of citizenship and political literacy, which are an essential part of any environmental education program. Indeed, John Huckle frames his two papers in terms of promoting political literacy and citizenship in the context of environmental issues. Huckle believes that geography can be used to develop students' critical awareness of existing social structures and their ability to engage and transform society (i.e. as social reconstructionism), a notion that is in accord with the aims of environmental education. McElroy's paper on political literacy challenges geography to prepare students for participation in society and provides guidelines for classroom implementation. Gough's paper, by suggesting alternative futures, also provides ideas for incorporating empowerment in school programs. The political literacy aspects of environmental education for Australian classrooms has not been explored fully to date. This volume provides a good starting point for some reflection on these aspects and on the problematic and political nature of environmental education.

Greenall, A. E. *Environmental Education in Australia: Phenomenon of the Seventies* (A Case Study in National Curriculum Development), Occasional Paper no. 7. Curriculum Development Centre, Canberra, 1981.

Case studies on national curriculum action in Australia are rare, so it is fortunate to find one about environmental education. This study was written by a participant in that development. It traces the development of environmental education in Australia as a national curriculum issue from its formal recognition in April 1970 to its inclusion as one of the nine essential areas of knowledge and experience in the CDC's core curriculum. The study focuses on the CDC as the major activist because it was to the CDC that educators looked for action during the 1970s. The development is explored at three levels: (1) as a sequence of events in time and space; (2) as a response to social, economic and educational pressures; and (3) as a product of individual initiative and action. The study argues that the development of environmental education has been problematic and subject to both party political and personal political posturing. The time span for the case study ends seven years ago, and the study concludes that environmental education as a phenomenon of the 1970s in Australia was counter-hegemonic to the action of Australian schools, but had been incorporated into the existing hegemony by the end of the decade. It provides a substantial base for interpreting the present status of environmental education in Australia.

Linke, R. D. (ed.). *Education and the Human Environment*. Curriculum Development Centre, Canberra.

This report of the 1975 Australian National Commission for the UNESCO Seminar on Education and the Human Environment is an important document. Indeed, the seminar could be seen as a key event in the legitimation of environmental education as a symbol of change in Australian education. Many of the papers presented at the seminar had lasting effects on the major activists in the development of environmental education in Australia. Of particular influence were the papers by Lawrence Stenhouse, William Hall and John Mayfield. These three papers challenged curriculum developers to produce materials which were 'good enough to stimulate teachers and to make them curious, but bad enough so that teachers will think they can do better and take over the ideas themselves' (p. 32). This is the challenge that Fensham and others bought to the Curriculum Development Centre Study Group on Environmental Education in 1977, and which provided a framework for the study group's recommendations. These speakers also argued that environmental education is not science, geography or something else, but rather that 'the unique contribution of environmental education should be in the area of problem solving and associated *decision making*, which in turn should lead to a willingness to *act*' (pp. 68–9). Educators are still coming to grips with this challenge. In addition to these keynote addresses, the report contains a summary of state education department position papers presented to the seminar (which provides a useful state-of-the-art perspective for 1975), working party reports on a number of topics, and supplementary and selected papers.

Environmental education and the question of gender: A feminist critique

Giovanna Di Chiro

Introduction

ON A GLOBAL scale, there is consensus that the earth and its inhabitants are in social and environmental peril. This is where the consensus ends, however, for there is equally widespread disagreement over the nature, causes and extent of the problems and the most appropriate and effective responses to them. This essay critically examines environmental education, one such 'appropriate response' to the global socio-environmental crisis. It advocates the adoption of a critical feminist perspective of environmental education to aid in the understanding and development of appropriate solutions to environmental problems.

Environmental education emerged in the early 1970s when the environmental movement was gaining momentum and vitality on a worldwide scale (see, for example, Stapp 1970; Disinger 1983; Robottom 1985). The international participants at the three major United Nations (UN) environmental conferences held that decade considered environmental education to be the most appropriate and hopeful response to the deterioration of quality of life and the environment (Fensham 1978). The aims of environmental education that emerged from the United Nations Educational, Scientific and Cultural Organization—United Nations Environmental Programme (UNESCO-UNEP) Intergovernmental Conference on Environmental Education in Tbilisi, USSR, in October 1977 were particularly ambitious in that they transcended a concern with the roles, objectives and guiding principles of environmental education and spelt out the need for an understanding of

> ... the epistemological and institutional structures that affect consideration of environment demands ... [and] ... the obstacles (epistemological, cultural or social) restricting access to educational messages and to their utilization. (UNESCO 1980, pp. 84, 93)

Put simply, the report from Tbilisi advocated a socially, culturally and epistemologically critical role for environmental education. Such a critical role would

> ... encourage careful analysis and awareness of the various factors involved in the situation [of the environment] ...
>
> All decisions regarding the development of society and the improvement of the lot of individuals are based on considerations, usually implicit, concerning what is useful, good, beautiful, and so on. The educated individual should be in a position to ask such questions as: Who took this decision? According to what criteria? With what immediate ends in mind? Have the long-term consequences been calculated? In short, he [sic] must know what choices have been made and what value-system determined them. (UNESCO 1980, p. 27)

It is clear that environmental education is at the same time a critique of the value components (the politics) of environmental decisions and actions, and itself a political enterprise making value judgments on who, what, where and how to educate for the environment. Like any form of education, environmental education is a social practice that aims to bring about changes and improvements in its field of action – in this case, education for an environmentally aware and active citizenry. It is essential, therefore, for environmental education to examine the dialectics of its practice. It must play a role in combatting environmental problems and also be self-critical of its role in sustaining the social structures and relations that cause or support those problems.

Such a critique could take a variety of paths. One direction could be an examination of the taken-for-granted views and processes of education that characterise environmental education programs and curricula (Robottom 1985). For example, most environmental education progams embrace traditional, bureaucratic and instrumentalist modes of curriculum development, pedagogy and educational change: they are generally teacher-directed, driven by centrally produced curricula and assessed by objectives-based criteria, all characteristics which are antithetical to the aims of environmental education.[1]

Another direction, which is explored more fully in this essay, is to re-examine the major substantive area of environmental education, that is, its environmental problem-solving focus. This leads to a critique of the concepts 'environment' and 'environmental problem' that are accepted and promulgated by proponents of environmental education. What would be the nature of such a critique?

The social nature of 'environment' and the 'environmental problem'

Firstly, let us look at the term 'environment'. The popular conception of the environment has become equated with nature and ecology despite the efforts of the early stages of the environmental movement (including the environmental education movement) to link the physical-ecological with the social, political and economic aspects of the world in which we live. Today's environmentalists have even adopted the symbolic colour of nature and refer to themselves as 'green'. A concern for the environment has, to all intents and purposes, become a concern for the restoration and protection of nature. The environmental education movement has evolved in a similar fashion, despite the highly politicised and socio-cultural intentions that emerged from the deliberations of the member states at the three UN conferences in the 1970s.

Green politics, which have become the orthodoxy of the modern environmental movement, have succeeded in creating the conception that nature or the physical environment directly shapes the social world. This view, sometimes referred to as 'ecological determinism' (Weston 1986), fails to recognise the dialectical relationship between the ecological and the social worlds and rejects the notion that the concept of 'environment' is socially constructed. It denies that

> . . . it is we, as a society, who shape our environment by deciding which social and economic priorities should prevail; we choose our environment rather than have it imposed upon us by 'nature'. Whether we live in the centre of a large city or on the edge of a forest, the physical environment starts at our front doors, making environmental issues those which are concerned with our surroundings – both physical and social – rather than those which are in some way related to 'nature'. (Weston 1986, p. 14)

The environment is what surrounds us, materially and socially. We define it as such by use of our own individual and culturally imposed interpretive categories, and it exists as the environment at the moment we name it and imbue it with meaning. Therefore, the environment is not something that has a reality totally outside or separate from ourselves and our social milieux. Rather, it should be understood as the conceptual interactions between our physical surroundings and the social, political and economic forces that organise us in the context of these surroundings. It is in this sense that we can say that the concept 'environment' is socially constructed. And if we view the environment as a social construct then we accept that certain qualities of it can be changed or transformed according to whichever social relationships are in operation.

If we view the environment as a social construct, we can also view the 'environmental problem' very differently:

> With so much poverty and social deprivation within our society it is increasingly difficult to accept the view that what we are faced with today is an 'ecological crisis' rather than a social or economic crisis. Indeed, such concepts as 'ecological crisis' tend to suggest that problems like acid rain, deforestation, and the spread of the deserts are somehow separate from the social world. People, although recognized by greens as the cause of such problems, are not seen as the main victims. The victim, as the phrase 'ecological crisis' suggests, is seen as being 'nature' — which relegates those suffering poverty, despair and hunger throughout the world to the periphery of their concern. Yet in fact it is people and not 'nature' who suffer the greatest hardship as a result of ecological damage. 'Nature', after all, will always reappear, albeit in a different form from that which has been destroyed; people, however, rarely live long enough to make up for the disruption and poverty caused to them when other people destroy their environment for personal economic gain. (Weston 1986, pp. 2–3)

Environmental problems are, therefore, social problems, caused by societal practices and structures, and only viewed or socially constructed as problems because of their effects on human individuals and groups (of course other living things and systems are also affected). This has broad implications for environmental educators because environmental education is strongly oriented to environmental problem solving. Before an environmental problem can be solved it must be adequately defined and understood so that an effective environmental education curriculum can be created and real solutions developed and applied.

This is not to say that an appreciation and sense of unity and connectedness with nature is not important to an understanding of our social world. Nor is it to imply that a strong philosophical base or nature-ecology paradigm would not contribute to environmental education's problem-solving goals. The point is that an adequate understanding of environmental problems requires that they be viewed as the products of contesting discourses, activities and interactions among human societies. Viewing them simply as issues of over-industrialisation or poor management of natural resources, which can be mitigated with well-designed 'technical fixes', ignores the real causes of the problems, and a narrow focus on nature or ecological balance as the primary 'victims' of the problems removes them from the messy realm of society and effectively depoliticises them.

The depoliticising of environmental problems may result in the oversimplification of the problem by framing it as a technical issue, the resolution of which simply requires new and more sophisticated technology, and the removal of the issue from the 'realm of possibility' in terms of ordinary people being able to do something to change the problem, i.e. it is left to the 'experts' and power-holders.

Environmental education, then, is a social practice which aims to educate for the environment with a problem-solving orientation. It follows that the examination of environmental problems requires a perspective that makes connections between these problems and social systems and structures. In other words, a social theory is required. Nancy Hartsock explains the significance of being clear and conscious about the social theories we hold:

> We must understand that theorizing is not just something done by academic intellectuals but that a theory is always implicit in our activity and goes so deep as to include our very understanding of reality . . . we can either accept the categories given to us by capitalist society or we can begin to develop a critical understanding of our world. If we choose the first alternative, our theory may forever remain implicit. In contrast, to choose the second is to commit ourselves to working out a critical and explicit theory. (Hartsock 1979, pp. 57–8)

The socially critical aims advanced at the UNESCO-UNEP conference at Tbilisi in 1977 require a social theory that critically examines the patterns and structures of social organisation in the environments in which we live. Without such a critical theory, environmental education maintains the assumptions and taken-for-granted beliefs that current global environmental conditions are a result of 'the natural order of things' or 'human nature'. Similarly, an uncritical acceptance of its educational assumptions and practices results in environmental education automatically adopting traditional views on education, at the same time as attempting to be an innovation.

The next section will explore the possibilities of a critical social theory that would be useful to environmental education's dual aims of environmental problem solving and educational change – a feminist critique.

A feminist perspective

A feminist analysis of society is one of a variety of critical social analyses that take a historical and political-economic view of human social relations and of the structures and problems that grow out of them. Other critical social analyses, which will not be discussed here, include Marxist socio-economic theory, critical reinterpretations of psychoanalytic theory, the critical theory of the Frankfurt School and radical humanistic-phenomenological theories.[2] Feminist theory differs from these in that it encompasses all components of the aforementioned theories, including class, race, age, etc., by illuminating the gendered construction of all such social categories. In my opinion, that difference makes it an essential analysis.

The question of gender is *the* critical benchmark of all forms of feminism (Eisenstein 1984). The term 'gender' is used to refer to socially and culturally created distinctions between femininity and masculinity (gentleness/toughness; intuitive/logical; passive/aggressive; body/mind; peaceable/violent), while the term 'sex' is used to refer to biological differences associated with reproduction between men and women. Society assigns roles, expectations and behaviours more or less arbitrarily to the two biological sexes. Feminism rejects this biological determinism – 'anatomy is destiny' – and maintains that gender differences are socially constructed and are therefore susceptible to transformation – that the sexes do not necessarily have to conform to their gender stereotypes. Furthermore, feminism argues that these socially constructed differences in gender roles between men and women systematically work to the advantage of men, so that the two sexes have unequal power, opportunities and social status.

So, feminism is not, as it is popularly understood, simply concerned with 'women's issues' and how to afford women equality of opportunity and participation (although these issues are important); it is an analysis of the gendered roles of men and women and an account of how these social constructions have shaped society and its institutions and practices throughout history. Hence, it is a study of men as well as of women. Feminism believes that men must recognise and understand the gendered construction of their position in society – that is, they must understand that they are located in the gendered category man and do not represent the generic category human (as our language might lead us to believe).

Feminism stresses that the two categories *masculine* and *feminine* are not simply opposite and equivalent concepts – that men and women must understand that the power and privilege bestowed upon the historically designated *masculine* gender and the inferior status likewise accorded the *feminine* gender are socially and culturally created irregularities and are not determined by 'natural law'.

Moreover, feminism is not (again, contrary to popular belief) an enterprise to retroactively 'add' or include women in patriarchal social systems, accounts of history or theoretical discourses. It is not concerned, for example, with 'tagging' women onto pre-existing systems as a 'corrective' of past omissions – Women and Natural Resources, Women and Development, Women and Peace. While feminism aims to understand the patriarchal (male-created and male-centred) underpinnings of society and how they created the 'invisibility' of women, it questions the adequacy of these assumptions, methods and frameworks for both understanding and living in the world.

Most importantly, feminism aims to explore ways in which current practices in society might be changed in order to dismantle those gendered structures and ideologies that subordinate women and oppress and exploit women and the other major social categories of race and class. (One form of feminism, eco-feminism, expands the notion of the victim of exploitative social values to include non-human life forms and eco-systems.)

Feminist theories do not aim to construct monolithic 'universals' or rigid orthodoxies with privileged truths and 'correct' methods. They do aim to challenge assumptions and *modus operandi* and to present alternative interpretations and discourses of 'reality' and what it means to be a human social being.

Although there is a wide variety of feminist perspectives, we can identify two broad approaches to the questions of why and how the gendered divisions in society have arisen and how these divisions provide insight into the forces that shape the state of the world, both socially and environmentally.

Radical feminism

The first approach, radical feminism (from the etymological meaning of 'root'), examines the interrelationships between the two genders and the ways in which these interrelationships operate to benefit men and subordinate women.[3] Radical feminists call this most fundamental or 'root' cause of social divisions and conflict 'patriarchy', and they believe that it explains why sex (a biological fact) becomes gender (a social phenomenon). As Kate Millett states:

> ... our society, like all other historical civilizations, is a patriarchy. The fact is evident at once if one recalls that the military, industry, technology, universities, science, political office, and finance – in short, every avenue of power within the society, including the coercive force of the police, is entirely in male hands. (Millett 1977, p. 25)

The subordination of women under patriarchy is a complex matter operating at different levels. Two distinct levels are the public level—male control of organisations, institutions and their rules, technology and culture—and the private, or personal, domestic level—male control of medical and political aspects of reproduction and the opportunities of women doing 'waged work' outside the home, thereby making them economically dependent on men. Radical feminists assert that the rule of men has not been enforced by visible coercion, but rather through the continued reproduction of an ideology that reinforces a separation between male and female roles, and then creates or sustains a set of beliefs about those roles.

The essential concept advanced by radical feminism, therefore, is not that men as a group consciously determine to dominate women, but that the institutional and hegemonic force of patriarchy grants men the privilege and benefits of social, economic and political power. Moreover, these gendered patterns of domination and subordination are embedded in our socio-cultural metaphors as woman is associated with 'nature' and man with 'culture'. This assertion will be elaborated in a later section.

Socialist feminism

The second major feminist analysis of society, socialist feminism, works toward linking gender relations to the wider social sphere and asserts that other factors, such as socio-economic class and race, interact with gender to produce complex patterns of dominance and subordination in society.[4] This analysis focuses mainly, although not exclusively, on the historical and socio-economic class factors that relate to the position of women under capitalist society. Specifically, socialist feminists aim to understand the relationships among the variety of class struggles over the control of the means of production (raw materials, machines, technology used in the manufacture of commodities) in a given capitalist society and the gendered nature of the social relations of production in that society. In other words, they seek to understand how the gendered construction of society under patriarchy interacts with other social forces of domination and subordination under capitalism. The sexual division of labour, which assigns to males the world of production and the paid workforce and to women the world of reproduction and the unpaid or underpaid workforce, becomes a key framework for analysis. This apparently neat (and 'natural') division of labour perpetuates certain patriarchal-capitalist values because the different types of labour are neither equally valued nor equally compensated, but close scrutiny demonstrates that the system appears neat only because many of its contradictions remain invisible:

> . . . if . . . women are primarily responsible for child care and domestic work in all capitalist societies (and in virtually all other existing societies as well), then women in their domestic role have an important, although unpaid, place in the maintenance of capitalism . . .
> Capitalists thus benefit not only from exploiting the labour of waged workers, but also indirectly from the cheap labour provided by women in reproducing the labour force. It is assumed that such labour is paid for out of men's wages. Men, although exploited, benefit from the fact that women are primarily responsible for domestic work and the family . . . not only are the isolation, and many of the stresses and strains involved in this domestic work, largely avoided by men, but women find themselves in a position where they, together with their children, are legally and economically dependent upon men.
> . . . many women not only play a vital part in the reproduction of the labour force, but they also do waged work—often in the home . . . in *theory* the woman does not need to work [for wages] because she is supported by her husband's wage, but in *practice* vast numbers have to do some kind of paid work in order to make ends meet. (Women and Geography Study Group of the Institute of British Geographers 1984, pp. 30–1)

This so-called 'double shift' of women (i.e. working to maintain the home and rear the family, as well as working for a wage) is one of the hidden structures of worldwide socio-economic systems which is becoming increasingly visible as the number of families headed by women expands yearly (*Women: A World Report* 1985). Socialist feminism focuses on the history and economics of the gendered workforce in capitalist societies and attempts to shed light on such current trends in global environmental problems.

The following sections will explore more fully a feminist perspective of environmental education by examining a feminist view of 'environment' and, briefly, a feminist view of education.

A feminist analysis of 'environment'

In an earlier section I stressed the importance of understanding that the concept 'environment' is a social construct. The rationale for a feminist critique of society was also briefly discussed and the notion of the gendered construction of the social world was suggested. How is, therefore, the social construct 'environment' gendered? The various feminist theories have tackled this issue in different ways.

Gender and patriarchal culture

Radical feminism focuses on the historical development of culture and how certain views of reality and the 'natural order of things' based on sexual divisions have become embedded in our socio-cultural discourses and practices. Rosemary Radford Ruether explains:

> Sexual symbolism is foundational to the perception of order and relationship that has been built up in cultures. The psychic organization of consciousness, the dualistic view of the self and the world, the hierarchical concept of society, the relation of humanity and nature, and of God and creation—all these relationships have been modeled on sexual dualism. (Ruether 1975, p. 3)

Ruether suggests that the melding of the world view of sexual dualisms and a hierarchical ordering of inferior and superior creates a cultural symbolic model of domination and subordination which legitimates the subjugation of the 'lower' race, class or sexual castes by the 'higher' ones. Animals, plants and nature are also relegated to the inferior end of the spectrum in our cultural metaphors.

These symbolic, psychical and religious roots of patriarchy form the foundation of radical feminism's concept of the nature–culture dichotomy. Man has been identified with culture—the mind; the intellectual, autonomous, spiritual, transcendent 'God the Father'. Woman has been identified with nature—the body; passivity, sensuality, dependency, fecundity, 'Mother Earth'. Through its genesis doctrine, the Judeo-Christian tradition decrees this Father-right of males' dominion over females, children, peoples of 'other' colour and 'other' religions, animals, plants and, finally, at the bottom of the hierarchy, nature (land, water, air). The language of domination and 'man' against 'nature'/woman is evident in our socio-cultural metaphors: 'conquer and subdue the wilds of nature', 'spoiling virgin wilderness', 'the rape of Gaia', 'manage, exploit, use, mastery over nature', 'you can't trust Mother Nature'. Ruether illustrates this point when she refers to *The Domination of Nature* (Leiss 1972) in a discussion of the effects of science and technology on the environment:

> . . . Francis Bacon [represents] the transition from the earlier mythic and religious roots of the concept of domination of nature to its modern scientific, technological expression

... the roots of the language of domination of nature [are] in social domination ... the 'master of nature' is imaged as a patriarchal despot whose subjugation of nature is expressed in the language of domination over women and slaves ...

The language is both that of despotism and that of sexual aggression. Nature is pictured as a fecund female slave whose 'children' are to be used by rulers by reducing her to a condition of total submission ... the ecological crisis and the collapse of faith in scientific technology in the twentieth century ... [are] the results of this relationship of 'use' of nature to social domination ... The productivity that resulted from the application of instrumentalist science to nature was fed into a magnification of the structures of social domination, rather than providing the basis for a postscarcity, equalitarian society. (Ruether 1975, pp. 186–7)

The radical feminist critique of the patriarchal dualism of nature (woman) versus culture (man) finds expression in the philosophy of eco-feminism. One of eco-feminism's central concerns is the historical division in Western societies of the notion of the unity of humans' essential male and female qualities into the polar opposite concepts of 'masculine' and 'feminine'. Eco-feminists believe that a dialectical relationship between the polar opposite masculine and feminine principles (Yin and Yang in Eastern philosophy) existed in ancient times. For example, the Egyptian deity Neith, who personified the eternal female and male principles in one form, was prominent in ancient civilisations (Stone 1976). At some point in history, sexual differentiation occurred in human societies, and each culture imposed its own values and definitions on 'masculine' and 'feminine'. Simultaneously these concepts were identified with biological maleness or femaleness. The reintegration of these polarities into the consciousness of society is the primary aim of eco-feminists, who believe that a society which views the individual as a natural synthesis of both masculine and feminine qualities would be more holistic, egalitarian and environmentally sound.

This type of radical feminism, which examines the connections between feminism, ecology and environmental problems, has positive aspects, but there are some difficulties, too. For example, consider these comments by Petra Kelly, the first woman to be elected head of the German Green (Ecologist) Party:

While women have increasingly discovered their own oppression in Western Europe, in the USA, in Australia and elsewhere, they have also learned to organise themselves and speak out against the oppression of others. There has been much consciousness raising. Political issues have become personal – and personal issues political ...

I have hope for the world ... because women all over the world are rising up, infusing the anti-nuclear, peace and alternative movements with a vitality and creativity never seen before.

... all our major problems: nuclear war, overpopulation, pollution, hunger, the desolation of the planet, the inequality among peoples ... [are] a crisis, *not* of information, but of *policy*. We cannot cope with all the problems that threaten us, while maximising profits ...

As things stand now, the people, especially women and children of the Third World are to perish first ...

In the last few years, I have also observed that women, through their downgrading have sought to raise their status at times by becoming part of the masculine world (cf. Mrs Thatcher, Indira Gandhi). When women fight for equal status with men, the danger is that one day they may become four star generals, build death technology, and join the front ranks in times of war ...

Coming to terms with and relating to the masculine within ourselves is a crucial part of our development as women, both collectively, and individually ...

Women must lose all their fears in speaking up, in demanding what is *theirs* and their children's. Only if we begin to rediscover our own nature, can we forge new ways, ways of wholeness, balance, decentralisation, preservation, mutual inter-dependence, co-operation, gentleness, non-possessiveness and soft energies.

. . . in order to stop living *against* the earth, in order to create technology that serves us and does not enslave us, we must reassert feminine values of wholeness, balance and harmony. It must become *impossible* for a small ruling class to monopolise the wealth from world resources, while transferring the social costs for the people in the form of poisoned air, water, soil and cells.

One of my greatest hopes is that men would *recover* the affective and nurturing roles with children and other people historically denied to them . . . and which has repressed the gentle humane side of males and shaped the male personality into that hyper-aggressiveness and antagonistic combativeness. (Kelly 1984, pp. 258–60, 62)

Although Kelly makes direct and clear connections between the historical gender division of society and ecological destruction, environmental problems and militarism, she falls into the common trap of 'false universalism'. Such universalism, characteristic of the radical/eco-feminist perspective, generalises the experience of all women, and ignores the differences of race, class and culture. All too often it gives rise to analyses that purport to speak about and on behalf of all women, black or white, poor or rich, thereby masking some of the economic and cultural structures which support sexism, racism, classism and environmental destruction. Implicit in this false universalism is the eco-feminist vision of the 'metaphysical' woman – the notion that women have a bond which is eternal, biological, historical and spiritual (Eisenstein 1984). Supporters of this view believe there is an inherent 'essence' of woman which embraces those feminine values of nurturing, gentleness, peaceableness and love of nature. But the effect of such a vision is deterministic in that it accepts gender divisions on the basis of biological sex and formulates woman as the 'other' (and, similarly, nature as the 'other', as in 'man versus nature').

When we examine the composition of social change organisations and activist groups working on disarmament, anti-nuclear issues, peace, environmental protection and education, we find them highly 'gendered' in favour of women (Strange 1983). Penny Strange suggests that we should ask why:

It is our vision and our practice of a new way to peace that makes women such an important force in the peace movement – not any 'natural pacifism' attributed to women. The common belief that women are by nature non-aggressive is itself part of the feminine stereotype of passivity, the complement to the idea that violence and war are 'natural' to men. Just as boys are initiated into the male club, so girls are taught to accept male dominance. They learn to distrust their own opinions, and their physical abilities: in place of confidence and assertion, they learn endurance and patience . . .

Women are not inherently nonviolent: they are traditionally oppressed, and as an oppressed group, have often turned their anger and violence in upon themselves. Nor are men inherently violent: they are traditionally and structurally dominant, and retain that dominance through the cultivation of toughness and violence. Women are not 'Earth Mothers' who will save the planet from the deadly games of the boys – this too is part of the support and nurture role that women are given in the world. Upon the support and silence of women has been built the male edifice of dominance, exploitation and war. (Strange 1983, pp. 26–7)

Some environmental educators emphasise the importance of the 'feminisation' (Ellyard 1981) of our war-oriented and anti-ecological societies, i.e. they say that society should value and incorporate the 'innate' gentle, creative, holistic and peace-loving properties of 'feminine' woman. Such values are virtuous and undoubtedly essential to the development of a new social and ecological order. But this deterministic view of social relations is dangerous because it suggests that male chemistry (testosterone-poisoning) causes war, destruction and decay of the Earth and that female chemistry (life-giving estrogen) will protect and save it. In other words, the gendered relations and structures of patriarchy come to be viewed as natural and, therefore, not subject to transformation. In this way, the possibility of men 'naturally' engaging in alternatives to war when resolving conflicts is effectively removed, and the burden of nurturing and peace-making is placed on women because such qualities are seen to be part of their 'female nature'.

Gender and socio-economic class

Another major analysis of how the concept 'environment' is gendered emerges from the socialist feminist perspective, which considers the resonances between gender and socio-economic class. This analysis takes a 'binocular approach', which considers how these structures of power – gender and class – have historically developed in interaction with each other. Connell et al. stress that the two categories do not operate in isolation:

> Sometimes people think of class relations as confined to the factory and gender relations to the family . . . This . . . is mistaken. There are gender relations inside factories, and there are class relations inside families and in the upbringing of children . . .
>
> They involve control by some people over others, and the ability of some groups to organize social life to their own advantage. As power is exercized and contested, social relations are organized and come to be in some degree a system . . .
>
> Both class and gender are *historical* systems, riddled with tension and contradiction, and always subject to change. Indeed it may be better to think of them as *structuring processes* rather than 'systems', that is, ways in which social life is constantly being organized (and ruptured and disorganized) through time. (Connell et al. 1982, p. 180)

How are the resonances between these two categories reflected in our critical analyses of environment and the environmental problem? This can be explored by looking at the connections between development and environment, which have worldwide implications. A class analysis alone has been applied in critical theorising about global environmental problems and political environmentalism (see, for example, Weston 1986; Porritt 1984; Schumacher 1973; Pepper 1984). Even in international environmental education, notions of 'North–South' (rich countries–poor countries) relations have been evoked to conceptualise the educational responsibilities and challenges facing developed and developing countries (Tuntawiroon 1986). Redclift shows how the environment and the environmental problem are perceived differently through the eyes of the poor in Third World countries:

> First, when we refer to 'the environment' in developing countries we are referring to something which has been produced by history, through struggles and exploitation, usually as part of the colonial and post-colonial accumulation process . . . It is important not to divorce the environment from its parts, especially the human populations whose productive activities have contributed to its evolution.
>
> Second, most . . . small-scale societies depend upon good ecological management to ensure future production. For . . . most 'peasant' or pastoralist groups, the viability of the 'natural' environment is a condition of their existence. There is no divorce between their 'culture' and their ecology; 'nature' as a social category, assumes importance in their . . . 'world view' . . .
>
> Third, the impact of capitalism in . . . 'less developed' countries implies contradictions for those with limited access to resources and power . . . Self-sufficiency in food production or energy is difficult when labour, especially that of women, has to be allocated to gaining cash or to meeting the exigencies of the market and the state. Under these cir-

cumstances poor people inevitably have greater recourse to their 'natural' environment – which acts as the focus of the household's attempt to reconcile the needs of the family with those of the market. (Redclift 1986, pp. 86–7)

By reflecting on this different view of the environment and the problems resulting from its 'use', it is easy to see how people from developing countries do not always display unequivocal commitment to environmental goals as they are perceived in the 'North'. The poor are often blamed for ecological degradation because they are forced into opposition with their own environments in the struggle for survival. A class analysis of the environmental crisis, therefore, is concerned with the role played by the socio-economic structures of international capital, trade relations between developed and developing countries, and large-scale, 'high-tech' agribusiness. The questions of gender relations and the patriarchial underpinnings of these structural elements are almost always omitted or relegated to insignificance in such environmental critiques. But when we examine the problem more critically, we find that it is neither simply a technical problem to be ameliorated by advanced technology, nor simply an economic problem to be eliminated solely by class redistribution of wealth.

In recent years, the flood of statistics generated by a variety of international aid, training and extension services has shown that the poor, specifically women and their children, are the main victims of the negative effects of transnational economic policies and their environmental consequences.[5] Consider these statements on the worldwide condition of women which were made at a UN General Assembly in 1980:

> Women suffer dual oppression of sex and class within and outside the family. The effects are strikingly apparent in the present world profile of women. While women represent 50 per cent of the world population, they perform nearly two-thirds of all working hours, receive only one-tenth of the world income and own less than 1 per cent of world property . . .
> Woman's work [has become] visible: her bearing and raising children, her sole responsibility for domestic work, her provision of most of the world's health care, her growing of half the world's food – all of this done for no wages – plus over a third of the world's paid labour too. (*Women: A World Report* 1985, p. 82)

Third World development planning and aid often ignores women because they are rendered 'invisible' by their domestic gender role and the sexual inequalities that devalue this role and obtain their labour free. Patriarchal culture, which enforces these differential gender roles, imposes social norms, taboos and practices which make it difficult, if not impossible, for women in developing countries or poor women in rich countries to undertake paid labour, own land for cultivation to earn a livelihood, carry and use cash, *not* have children, reduce childbearing and childcare responsibilities, use contraception, gain an education, procure development loans and other forms of aid, and become involved in decision making that affects their and their children's welfare (*Women: A World Report* 1985). Hence the phrase 'the feminisation of poverty', which refers to the UN's recognition of the disproportionate increase of poverty in the world's women (Caldecott & Leland 1983; *Women in the World: An International Atlas* 1986).

Applying a feminist critique to an environmental problem

This section considers two examples of how the dimensions of an environmental problem might be approached using a feminist analysis. Such an approach has significance for environmental education's case study orientation in environmental problem-solving activities in the classroom. The first example, a brief account of an environmental problem in a village in India, clearly shows how the power structures of gender and class are linked to environmental issues.

The Chipko Movement

> In a remote village in Northern India called Reni, nestled in the Garhwal mountains of the Himalayan range, a group of women and children were doing an unusual thing. Hugging trees. They were resorting to Chipko, which means to hug, to prevent trees from being felled. With their arms wrapped around the trees, the women and children cried: 'The forest is our mother's home, we will defend it with all our might.' The women and children stopped about 70 lumberjacks from the forest contractors who were ready to fell the trees.
>
> This event, which happened in 1974, marked the beginning of the now well known Chipko Andolan, or movement, which forced the state government to set up a committee to investigate the concerns of women. The committee reported that about 12 000 kilometres of the sensitive watershed area of the Alkananda Valley were endangered. The government then declared this area out of bounds for felling. (Anand 1983, p. 182)

Why were these women particularly concerned about the fate of these trees? They were concerned because they have experiential understanding of the importance of natural resources in their lives. Only four years before this demonstration a catastrophic flood had swept through the valley and washed away homes, bridges, cattle and their major source of timber and fuel. The government responded by establishing a reafforestation plan, replacing the indigenous oak with the faster growing and commercially valuable pine.

Pine, unlike oak, was a cash crop exploited by forest contractors and speculators, especially during the Indo-Chinese conflict in the 1960s and 1970s when the timber was needed for roads, bridges and other facilities demanded by the army. Men were encouraged to join the army, thereby leaving the women to support the village alone. Constrained by their domestic role in the sexual division of labour, the women found this a near impossible task. They were responsible not only for their domestic work, but also for the work usually done by the men of the village. Some of this work, however, was denied the women because it was culturally prohibited on the basis of their sex. For example, women are not allowed to own land so they could not produce a cash crop to earn money to buy food, and in some villages women were prohibited from even possessing cash.

In their efforts to sustain the village, they came face to face with the environmental consequences of bad development planning. For hundreds of years the leaf litter and the massive root systems of the indigenous oak trees had produced a nutrient-rich humus and a water catchment, providing fertile land and water for the local community. The acidic soil of the commercial pine forests, however, had rendered the valley's land unfit even for subsistence needs, so for many food was hard to come by. Women in India are primarily responsible for the production, processing and storage of food, the collection of fuel and water, and the care of the domestic animals. Their main source of fuel—wood—was tied up in the holdings of the timber companies or the government, so they had to walk five to ten miles a day to collect firewood for cooking and fodder for cattle. When firewood became unavailable they were forced to use animal dung, which further depleted the local soil of much needed nutrients. The women engaged in 'Chipko' (which has a long cultural tradition in India) to protect the trees with their bodies in an attempt to prevent the logging company's deforestation of their environment. They were experiencing personally the effects of environmental degradation—it was a question of survival (Monk & Williamson-Fien 1986).

The women had no voice in the community's decision-making process because decision making was a male privilege sustained by patriarchy. Patriarchy takes different forms in different cultures. In the case of Third World development programs, planning without foresight or an adequate understanding of the culture's gender relations often results in the most oppressive aspects of the sexual division of labour being maintained and even exacerbated. As women are the subservient caste in society, they and their children suffer the hardships of environmental deterioration or bad development planning. This is demonstrated clearly in the Chipko case because the West's patriarchal devaluing of 'women's work' in development programs helps men to earn wages or grow cash crops while ignoring and creating difficulties in women's vital subsistence farming practices.

The women of Reni and the Chipko were not subject to the laws of purdah (the Indian custom of incarcerating women to hide them from public view), although nearby in certain villages in Bangladesh women 'under the veil' would suffer severe punishment if they were seen in public, even when carrying out their domestic chores. This becomes a problem when the village water supply runs low and the men refuse to share in the 'women's work' of water-carrying. One environmental problem resulting from this situation is the spread of disease throughout the village when households have insufficient water to maintain hygiene.

Women living under purdah face significant obstacles in initiating change that would improve their situation, although change is occurring through modernisation, with some regions eliminating purdah. The women of the Chipko movement were not passive and unresisting, and their efforts met with some success. Examples such as these, in a Third World context, demonstrate how the injustices of gender inequality (especially among poor women) are so closely tied to problems of the environment.

Indian scholar and activist Anita Anand stresses the need to look critically at the fundamental causes of socio-environmental problems:

> The example of Chipko reveals that leadership in some of the villages has been supportive of the women. In other villages, the husbands and sons have mixed feelings. The men complain that women have become domineering, unfeminine and bold, and one complained that his wife had stopped making him tea! The issue is one of control. As Chandi Prasad Bhatt, one of the male leaders of the movement says, 'Control by local people yes, but who among local people: men or women?'
>
> Controlling mechanisms in movements like Chipko are a carryover from norms in society at large. Male privilege in decision-making cuts across races, classes and cultures. The institutionalisation of patriarchy and hierarchy are rampant and manifest themselves in all levels of society. Role definitions as ascribed to men and women further exacerbate the situation, when self-confidence and worth are being questioned. Expectations of what either sex does best undermine and dehumanise the real potential of both women and men.
>
> A study of the needs and perceptions of women and men could lead us to look at the way both sexes are socialised into accepting what the world means to them . . .
>
> Introduction of basic technologies to meet the needs of poor people, where investment opportunities and decisions are made by and controlled by men, will meet with resistance unless the question of sexual equity is dealt with. The social and religious mores, which have created and reinforced stereotypes of the roles of men and women in society, may have to change first. (Anand 1983, pp. 184–5, 186)

Anand asserts that the issue is not simply the need to reform the exploitative practices of the international economy (where developing nations are forced into opposition with their environments in order to survive on a subsistence basis or satisfy export
markets) but is of greater complexity. Underlying socio-economic class structures are
other social forces that work against improvements in these unjust situations throughout
the world. What is needed, says Anand, is an effective way to analyse these forces to
bring about social and environmental change:

> Some social scientists have argued that equality between classes is a prerequisite for growth.
> Feminists would argue that no 'real' growth is possible without a re-examination of power
> relations between the sexes as well. The contribution of feminism to the environmental
> and development movements is the insistence that all forms of domination must be eradi-
> cated and that the living relations of subordination be a central problem for study, reflection
> and action for change. (Anand 1983, p. 187)

Although the Chipko example illuminates the effects of gender inequality on the
environment in a Third World/Eastern context, it must be emphasised that the injustices
of gender oppression are not only problems of the Third World or 'other ethnics'. In
advanced capitalist, Western countries, the extremes of women's subordination, such
as purdah, do not exist *per se* in their socio-cultural practices and discourses. In more
subtle forms, however, the inferior status and marginal location of women (especially
poor women in rich countries) is just as potent and is most strikingly thrown into relief
in times of social, economic and ecological (i.e. environmental) deterioration. The second
example of applying a feminist analysis to an environmental problem focuses on a 'First
World' context and examines the environmental effects of the increasing nuclearisation of society.

The anti-nuclear and peace movements

The proliferation of the nuclear fuel cycle and its relation to the threat of nuclear war
are considered by many to be the most serious environmental problems of the modern
age. A meltdown at a nuclear plant or a nuclear war would cause large-scale human
and ecological devastation or the annihilation of life as we know it on the planet Earth.

In the past two decades an unprecedented number of educational, political and
activist groups concerned with addressing such environmental problems have emerged
throughout the world. The overwhelming majority of these groups have been established and are run by women, and many operate with a membership that is exclusively
women – Women Against Nuclear Energy, Women Oppose the Nuclear Threat, Women
For Survival, Women for Life on Earth, Greenham Common Women's Peace Camp,
Women's International League for Peace and Freedom, Mothers for Peace, etc. (Strange
1983).

Once again we need to ask, why women? What is the relationship between this
all-encompassing environmental problem – the dangers of nuclearism – and the interests
of women on such a global scale? In this case we turn our attention to a movement
that is characterised largely (although not exclusively) by the involvement of women
of white, middle-class, Western societies. Most of the women involved, unlike women
of Third World countries, are not suffering from apparent poverty and material depri-
vation, but, as for the women of the Chipko movement, the issue is nevertheless one
of survival. Although the question of survival in the two worlds is different in nature –
the Third World predicament is more immediate and basic – there are common threads.
The subordination of women under the institution of patriarchy in any society creates

greater problems for women in the event of worsening social and environmental conditions. As we have noted, patriarchy is expressed differently in different cultural contexts. We shall now look at the way it operates in the women's anti-nuclear and peace movements in Australia.

The Australian link in the international proliferation of nuclear technology and warfare is in the production of uranium (a raw material necessary in the development of nuclear bombs) and the granting of permits for the installation of US military bases on Australian soil. Why are women in Australia concerned with breaking this link in the nuclear chain?

Women in Australia, and worldwide, are making the connections between the social relations and structures of patriarchy and a violent, war-like society. In other words, women have put sexism on the agenda in the anti-nuclear and peace movements. There is growing recognition that the violence against women – rape, assault, domestic violence, exploitation, pornography – and the violence of war, the arms race and the ultimate destruction of the earth have common roots in the patriarchal cosmology of separation, hierarchy and dominance.

It has long been accepted by peace activists that the violence of racism and poverty are as real and essential 'peace' issues as disarmament and anti-nuclear technology (Weston 1986). For the majority of people in the world whose lives are dictated by the daily routine of exhaustive manual or menial labour and drudgery in order to simply feed and shelter themselves and their children, the threat of nuclear annihilation remains remote and irrelevant. The more immediate and tangible problems of unemployment, substandard housing, scarcity of food, insanitary water supplies and racial or sexual harrassment form the crux of their environmental crises. As Martin Luther King explained, peace is not simply the absence of war, and it means nothing without the commitment to goodwill, 'brotherhood' and social justice.

It is such a peace, a 'green-peace', for which women in Australia and throughout the world are struggling – a 'peace' that also includes the social justice of 'sisterhood' in its aims. Women's peace and anti-nuclear groups are saying that the effects of the nuclearisation of the world are being felt right now. The ultimate destruction of the planet Earth has not happened, yet there is widespread ecological and social destruction, in effect a 'nuclear war', occurring in our local environments. Levene elaborates:

> There has been a slow – sometimes painfully slow – but developing consciousness . . . that people can suffer, be exploited or genetically damaged long before the bombs have gone off . . .
>
> Since 1946 some 250 nuclear devices have been detonated by both east and west in the Pacific (to say nothing of those tested elsewhere), with inevitably disastrous and hideous effects on people's health – most strikingly on women's ability to conceive normal, healthy children. The detonations these days are underground, but this has not prevented the building of bases, the mining of uranium in nearby Australia, or the wider and more general carving up of the area as if it was just so much real estate for military purposes. It is important to realize, however, that these developments are not simply a question of nuclear weapons, nuclear bases, or even nuclear dumping. Taking over areas of the globe for political, strategic or economic reasons – or more usually an amalgam of all three – regardless of the nuclear element, means the degradation and marginalisation of people's working and living environments, even sometimes their complete removal. (Levene 1986, p. 41)

Women in Australia are making the connections between the Australian 'link in the nuclear chain' (uranium mining and housing military bases) and both the potential of nuclear war and the growing atmosphere of violence resulting from the nuclearisation of Australian society. A nuclear society, they say, 'will only increase the sexism which women suffer' (*Chain Reaction* 1978, p. 16) The following are some examples of how an expanded uranium mining industry would adversely affect women in Australia[6]:

- Government subsidies to uranium mining would reduce government expenditures for human services, welfare, child support, etc. The majority of the recipients of these government services are women.

- The increase of capital investment in the uranium mining industry with the government's concomitant inequitable taxation of mining companies results in less total government revenue. Again, less money is available for human services, and women and their children are the primary losers.

- Government policy of 'trading our way out of trouble' results in an emphasis on primary industry (especially mining) to the detriment and reduction of 'inefficient' industries such as manufacturing. These industries employ mainly women, especially migrant women.

- The over-valuing of a resource industry such as uranium mining results in the devaluing of non-productive, non-tradeable industries such as education, welfare, healthcare, etc. These are traditionally women's industries.

- The jobs creation scheme outlined by the uranium lobby is considered to be the most expensive in history, at $500 000 invested per job. Very few of these jobs are intended for women.

- Many uranium deposits lie under Aboriginal sacred lands. Aboriginal women (and men) would suffer cultural destruction with an expanded uranium mining industry, not only as a result of the poisoning and degradation of the land itself, but through the influx of mining 'company towns' bringing problems of alcoholism, rape and syphilis. Aboriginal women have minimal 'sacred space' within their own culture's patriarchal constraints, so the destruction of these limited sites for women means disrupting Aboriginal women's practice of dreaming.

- It is said that the 'erosion of a citizen's liberties increases exponentially in direct proportion to a country's involvement in the nuclear fuel cycle' (*Chain Reaction* 1978, p. 11). This would affect both women and men, but in the patriarchal structures which control our society, women already suffer reduced civil liberties.

- Directly related to uranium mining in Australia is the housing of US military bases. Women are used as sexual bait by the business community to extract the big dollars from servicemen on R and R. (Overseas, women in Guam and the Philippines have had to resort to prostitution as their only means of making a living because the self-sufficiency and autonomy of their islands is broken down by the foreign military base take-overs.)

In the earlier example of the Chipko movement, we saw women of the Third World struggling for their material well-being and even their mere existence. In this 'First World' example, women (mainly of the white middle-class, but on behalf of poor women in rich countries as well) are fighting against the accelerating nuclear treadmill in Australia which threatens to alienate or impoverish them further, or ultimately to destroy the Earth and everything they have created and worked for. Applying a feminist analysis to these two environmental issues illustrates how environmental destruction and nuclearisation extends the oppression of women and, moreover, shows that challenging these problems involves challenging the wider society's ideological, institutional, economic and cultural factors that sustain women's oppression.

This is why women's peace and anti-nuclear groups throughout the world are steadily increasing and are seen to be posing a serious threat. By their actions, including demonstrations, civil disobedience, lobbying, educational activities and consciousness-raising, they are challenging the future of patriarchal society. Poet Joan Cavanagh (1984, pp. 257–8) expresses this challenge with her searing words:

I am a dangerous woman

I am a dangerous woman
Carrying neither bombs nor babies
Flowers or molotov cocktails.
I confound all your reason, theory, realism
Because I will neither lie in your ditches
Nor dig your ditches for you
Nor join your armed struggle
For bigger and better ditches.
I will not walk with you nor walk for you,
I won't live with you
And I won't die for you
But neither will I try to deny you
Your right to live and die.
I will not share one square foot of this earth with you
While you're hell-bent on destruction
But neither will I deny that we are of the same earth,
born of the same Mother
I will not permit
You to bind my life to yours
But I will tell you that our lives
Are bound together
And I will demand
That you live as though you understand
This one salient fact.

I am a dangerous woman
because I will tell you, sir,
whether you are concerned or not,
Masculinity has made of this world a living hell
A furnace burning away at hope, love, faith, and justice,
A furnace of My Lais, Hiroshimas, Dachaus.
A furnace which burns the babies
You tell us we must make,
Masculinity made Femininity
Made the eyes of our women go dark and cold,
sent our sons—yes sir, *our* sons—
To War
Made our children go hungry
Made our mothers whores
Made our bombs, our bullets, our 'Food for Peace,'
    our definitive solutions and first strike policies
Yes sir
Masculinity broke women and men on its knee
Took away our futures
Made our hopes, fears, thoughts and good instincts
'irrelevant to the larger struggle.'

And made human survival beyond the year 2000
An open question.
Yes sir
And it has possessed you.

I am a dangerous woman
because I will say all this
lying neither to you nor with you
Neither trusting nor despising you.
I am dangerous because
I won't give up, shut up, or put up
    with your version of reality.
You have conspired to sell my life quite cheaply
And I am especially dangerous
Because I will never forgive nor forget
Or ever conspire
To sell yours in return.

The power to make decisions about planning, policies, legislation and the economics of environmental issues and practices is overwhelmingly in men's control. If we integrate the radical feminist and the socialist feminist perspectives of the nature of the environmental problem we find that gender relations (in association with race and class) play a significant role in societies' cultural metaphors and norms of environmental practice (the ideological underpinnings of society) and in the power structures that control and sustain environmental practice (the political-economic underpinnings of society).

Case studies such as the Indian Chipko movement and the Australian anti-nuclear and peace movements are examples of activities appropriate for a critical environmental education curriculum for teacher education. In a classroom context, environmental issues and activies commensurate with the level and needs of the students would be called for. Depending on the educational situation, pragmatic concerns or pedagogical decisions about environmental education curricula would require the study of environmental issues of a much smaller scale and perhaps of a more local concern than the two previously addressed. Whichever level of analysis is undertaken – more local or more global – it is important to understand how environmental problems are interrelated.

Environmental education reconstructed

A feminist perspective of environmental education offers a more complete analysis of environmental problems and therefore a better understanding of those problems and their potential solutions. Such an analysis is political, in that it examines how power relations (in, for example, gender, class, race) shape the world in which we live; it asserts that the 'polity' (human social world) determines and controls how this social world is and has been historically constructed and organised, and hence refutes the myth that the past and present state of the world is a 'natural' and therefore justifiable progression. Moreover, environmental education's analysis of socio-environmental problems is political in that it believes that if human social relations create the problems they can also change and improve them.

Here we return to our initial premise about the mission of environmental education as it was formulated at Tbilisi. The 75 UNESCO-UNEP member states (most of which were classified as Third World or developing countries) clearly and systematically outlined the growing list of 'symptoms' of worldwide environmental problems. An initial analysis of the nature of these problems was proposed by conference participants, focusing on questions of conflicting values and their political implications. In this essay, this analysis was expanded to include a feminist perspective of how environmental problems are gendered. What should be the role of environmental education in responding to these problems? And what does it mean to teach environmental education?

Once again, we should evoke the recommendations from Tbilisi – environmental education should be problem-solving oriented and deal with values and how they serve to support certain environmental decisions over others. Let us first reiterate the major points of the preceding sections.

- I have argued that the environmental problem is socially constructed and should be viewed as a *social problem* – this elevates the concept from the technical domain to the realm of power and social relations, and so renders it amenable to a social critique, not simply a technological 'fix'.

- I have discussed the need for environmental education to engage in a *social critique* of environmental problems and those social relations and structures that perpetuate values and ideologies that sustain social/environmental problems. A feminist critique was proposed.

- I mentioned the need for environmental education to also engage in *self-criticism* in order to understand how it is responsible as an educational enterprise for maintaining certain 'un-environmental' values and ideologies.

At this point it is important to reconsider the political nature of education generally and environmental education specifically. The argument that education and teaching are political practices has been presented in Ian Robottom's essay in this book (see also Apple 1979; Freire 1985; Berlak & Berlak 1981). Robottom argues that traditionally uncritical practices of education and teaching tend to encourage teachers to adopt the role of technicians through whom appropriate and necessary socio-cultural knowledge is channelled by means of the curriculum. It follows that students are viewed as vacuous, passive recipients of this flow of wisdom. By accepting the appropriateness of curricula, teachers inadvertently instil those social values and norms that are inherent in the particular curriculum. As most curricula are centrally produced (external to the school and its specific needs), those implicit values reflect the interests of those who develop and select curricula.

In a similar fashion, most curricula in schools maintain the gender inequalities of the wider society, thus supporting the socialisation process which maintains the dominance of boys and the subordination of girls. The gender analysis of education and schooling is well documented and will not be elaborated here (see Spender 1982; Porter 1986; Blackburn 1984). Briefly, included in the feminist analysis of educational social relations are: (1) the concept of the 'invisibility' of women and women's experience in curricula; (2) the notion of 'male-as-norm' and female as different, and therefore deviant and inferior; and (3) the role of education and schools in the socialisation of girls and boys into society's sexual division of labour. Clearly, environmental education must examine not only its content – the environmental problem – but also its process of educating for a socially and environmentally just world.

The teacher of environmental education is, therefore, involved in negotiating, developing and practising curricula that will either maintain the status quo and reproduce its accompanying set of social values and ideologies or create the conditions for a teaching–learning environment that will promote a socially critical perspective of the environment and of solutions to its associated problems.

Towards a feminist environmental education

A feminist perspective of environmental education, integrating gender with class, offers a social critique that sheds light on the causes and definitions of environmental problems and the educational forms that would appropriately respond to them. In this essay I have stressed the need for environmental education to engage a critical social theory to inform, guide and transform its practice in the name of authentic environmental change. Specifically, I have argued for the importance of applying a feminist critique of the ideology of gender to the major substantive area of environmental education; that is, to the environmental problem. Similarly, we could examine the education features of environmental education through a feminist lens, exploring not only gender in education but also the process of constructing a feminist pedagogy which attempts to recast and transform our oppressive and unjust social constructs and practices. The particulars of such a task are beyond the scope of this essay, but I would like at least to outline how the practice of environmental education could benefit from feminist processes.

The practice of environmental education, as discussed earlier, is political because it is individuals and groups of people who make the decisions, based on their interests and values, regarding what, where and how environmental education will be taught. Moreover, feminism provides a social critique that illuminates the gender-based politics of the environment and of education. Robottom's essay in this book presents a critique of the traditional characteristics of education and environmental education as it has been realised over the years. Among these traditional characteristics are the positivistic assertion that social reality is objectively constituted, the view that education could be value-free, and the 'bureaucratic rationality' of RDDA (research, development, dissemination, adoption) curriculum development practices. Such traditional views of education tend to depoliticise the practice of environmental education and maintain the 'un-environmental' values of the status quo. Feminist forms of education and feminist pedagogical styles engage a similar critique and aim to construct alternative forms of education which redress the gender bias underpinning traditional education. Both environmental education and feminist forms of education (which find expression, in part, in the women's studies movement—see Culley & Portuges 1985) are political in nature, and have similarities in their philosophies and practices. Both are committed to a problem-solving orientation, interdisciplinary practices, social/environmental change, making process as important as content, action orientation, non-competitive group collaboration, democratic management of the teaching–learning environment, and empowerment to change one's life and act according to one's values.

If we recognise the politicised character of feminist and environmental education, how do we teach in a socially critical mode and remain aware of the ways in which we, as teachers, perpetuate values, beliefs and behaviours that are unjust and 'un-environmental'? How do we go about the practice of developing and improving curricula so that they are more educational in promoting the feminist/environmental education goals of critical awareness, empowerment and action for socio-environmental change?

Feminist forms of education would require that direct participants in educational practices be involved in activities to change and improve them. This can be accomplished by researching or self-monitoring the 'fit' of our social theories with our social practices. Such a 'participant/self-reflective' research approach would, I believe, greatly benefit environmental education development.

Feminist processes in environmental education curriculum development and reform would begin by recognising the importance of personal, subjective experience in understanding social reality. This does not mean simply a concern with what goes on inside our heads and the psychology of our inner thoughts; it entails a recognition that because we are social beings, it is also our social actions and reactions which should be central to a study of the development and practice of environmental education. In other words, a feminist view of environmental education improvement would require a form of 'inquiry' or 'research' that aims to understand and change environmental education issues and actions and is undertaken by those actors directly involved in environmental education practice.

Teachers (and students) of environmental education, therefore, are the appropriate researchers into environmental education practice and development. If we recall our feminist discussions of the gendered construction of hierarchy models of society, we can apply them to the social relations of education. Teachers, most of whom are women, are in the subordinate ranks of the education system (students are even lower in status but are seen as the recipients of the delivery system) and are traditionally the 'researched' not the 'researchers' of educational practices. But they are the so-called 'practitioners' of education, and who would know better the successes and failures of an environmental education curriculum? Teachers are excluded from the development and change processes in environmental education research and often feel that they do not possess the power or skills to be the instigators and producers of environmental education reform. The feminist perspective of participant-research believes that the relationship between our theory and practice of environmental education is mediated and articulated by understanding the connections and contradictions existing in what we do and what we think. Stanley and Wise illustrate how our discourses and practices maintain certain social structures and relations (for example, sexist ones) and work against change:

> Words, sentences, writing styles, ways of presenting arguments, arguments themselves, criticism, all these are part and parcel of masculinist culture. They are among the artefacts of sexism, and their use structures our experience before we can even begin to examine it, because they provide us with how we *think* as well as how we *write* . . . Sexism isn't discriminatory practices in employment and education, nor even the domestic division of labour. At its root sexism is a set of practices, contextually located and daily enacted, which fix us within them . . . sexism provides us not only with a vocabulary but also the structures through which we think, through which we conceptualize and enact 'society'. We can't break out of the circle until we can conceptualize 'outside of the circle'; and to do this requires new ways of conceptualizing; but to do this requires a different 'language', a different set of ways of structuring the world . . .
>
> Of course it isn't quite like this. The social world is neither so determinate nor so relentlessly sexist as this—but that it is presented as such is an important feature of the means by which sexism is perpetuated. To see that it *can* be changed, and that anyway people aren't so stereotyped as we're told that they are, is to begin to change it. But *how* we change it, how we break out of the circle—as well as whether we recognize that it is there to be broken out of—matters. (Stanley & Wise 1983, p. 183)

How do we bring about change? Educational reform occurs when we make committed, informed (theory) changes to educational experiences and activities (practice). Stanley and Wise offer a starting point for making changes in our thinking and acting to overcome gender oppression:

> If we are to resist oppression, then we need the *means* to do so. The means to resist oppression, we believe, are to be found where all of our oppressions are themselves to be found. Without knowing *how* oppression occurs we cannot possibly know *why* it occurs; and without knowing how and why it occurs we cannot find out how to avoid its occurrence, how it is that liberation might be achieved. Liberation has to start somewhere; we cannot leap into a liberated world overnight. We must necessarily effect many small liberations in many small and apparently insignificant aspects of our lives, or we shall never begin 'the revolution'. (Stanley & Wise 1983, p. 167)

Environmental education may not make claims to 'begin the revolution' with the politicisation of an environmentally active citizenry, but the recommendations that emerged at Tbilisi certainly urged moves in this direction. What are the means available to environmental education practitioners to unite their theory and practice and to bring about the necessary transformations in the environmental and educational qualities of environmental education? Feminist forms of education argue that people need to engage in critical inquiry (research), not only into the meanings of their own oppression but also into the institutional and broader social forces which have an impact on their thinking and acting. Action research is a form of self-critical and socially critical research which embraces many feminist principles and has been historically prominent in educational reform. Carr and Kemmis explain the aims of action research:

> There are two essential aims of all action research activity: to *improve* and to *involve*. Action research aims at improvement in three areas: firstly, the improvement of a *practice*; secondly, the improvement (or professional development) of the *understanding* of the practice by its practitioners; and thirdly, the improvement of the *situation* in which the practice takes place.
> The aim of *involvement* stands shoulder to shoulder with the aim of *improvement* . . . those involved in the practice being considered are to be involved in the action research process in all its phases of planning, acting, observing and reflecting. As an action research project develops, it is expected that a widening circle of those affected by the practice will become involved in the research process . . .
> What are the minimal requirements for action research? It can be argued that three conditions are individually necessary and jointly sufficient for action research to be said to exist: firstly, a project takes as its subject-matter a social practice, regarding it as a strategic action susceptible of improvement; secondly, the project proceeds through a spiral of cycles of planning, acting, observing and reflecting, with each of these activities being systematically and self-critically implemented and interrelated; thirdly, the project involves those responsible for the practice in each of the moments of the activity, widening participation in the project gradually to include others affected by the practice, and maintaining collaborative control of the process. (Carr & Kemmis 1983, pp. 154–5)

Action research incorporates the *feminist* principles of *the importance of valuing personal experience* (practitioners' self-reflection on educational practices and interpretive categories), *consciousness-raising in the context of a social group* (collaborative critical communities of educational practitioners), *an essentially socially critical impulse* (a reappraisal of the taken-for-granted, historically and culturally embedded beliefs about education and pedagogy), *a social action/change towards a social justice orientation* (changing educational practices, thereby effecting the transformations necessary to realise the emancipatory aims of education).

There are parallels between the aims and processes of environmental education and those of feminist forms of education and action research's participant-inquiry approach to educational change. Action research is an appropriate form of critical inquiry that would be useful to environmental educators for the development and improvement of their environmental education practice.

In this essay I have endeavoured to present a view of the problematic nature of environmental education. When we look below the surface, we find that there is no consensus about what it means to practice 'good' environmental education, nor about the processes and fundamental aims of environmental education. In the social world of education, environmental education practice is a political activity and is therefore subject to the conflicts of values, ideologies and decision-making processes concerning appropriate environmental education curricula and pedagogy.

Environmental education, then, cannot disregard these contested areas, but must make use of its essential problematic quality to advance its aims of socio-environmental change through education. To this end, I have argued that environmental education should embrace a political perspective of the environment (a feminist critique), as well as a political perspective of education (a socially critical impulse) and of educational development and change (an action research approach).

Notes

1 This critique is presented in Ian Robottom's essay in this book.
2 For example, see the writings of Marx, Althusser, Derrida, Lacan, Habermas, Marcuse, Foucault, Greene and Suransky.
3 Some readings in radical feminism include Daly (1978), Eisenstein (1984) and Morgan (1984).
4 Some readings in socialist feminism include Eisenstein (1979), Mitchell (1971) and Rowbotham, Segal & Wainwright (1979).
5 The first worldwide study of the status of women was compiled by Boserup (1970).
6 These examples are based on a personal communication from Anne Marie Delahunt, Canberra, ACT and *Chain Reaction* 1978.

References

Anand, A. (1983), 'Saving trees, saving lives: Third World women and the issue of survival', in L. Caldecott & S. Leland (eds), *Reclaim the Earth: Women speak out for Life on Earth*, The Women's Press, London.

Apple, M. W. (1979), *Ideology and Curriculum*, Routledge & Kegan Paul, London.

Berlak, A., & Berlak, H. (1981), *Dilemmas of Schooling: Teaching and Social Change*, Methuen, London.

Blackburn, J. (1984), 'Schooling and injustice for girls', in D. Broom (ed.), *Unfinished Business: Social Justice for Women in Australia*, Allen & Unwin, Sydney.

Boserup, E. (1970), *Women's Role in Economic Development*, St Martin's Press, New York.

Caldecott, L. , & Leland, S. (eds) (1983), *Reclaim the Earth: Women speak out for Life on Earth*, The Women's Press, London.

Carr, W., & Kemmis, S. (1986), *Becoming Critical: Knowing Through Action Research* (ECT432/732 *Action Research in Curriculum*), 2nd edn, Deakin University, Vic.

Cavanagh, J. (1984), 'I am a dangerous woman', in Cambridge Women's Peace Collective, *My Country is the Whole World: An Anthology of Women's Work on Peace and War*, Pandora Press, London.

Chain Reaction (1978), **3**(4).

Connell, R. W., Ashenden, D. J., Kessler, S., & Dowsett, G. W. (1982), *Making the Difference: Schools, Families and Social Division*, Allen & Unwin, Sydney.

Culley, M., & Portuges, C. (eds) (1985), *Gendered Subjects: The Dynamics of Feminist Teaching*, Routledge & Kegan Paul, Boston, Mass.

Daly, M. (1978), *Gyn/ecology: The Metaethics of Radical Feminism*, Beacon Press, Boston, Mass.

Disinger, J. (1983), 'Environmental education's definitional problem', *Informational Bulletin 2*, SMEAC Information Reference Center, Columbus, OH.

Eisenstein, H. (1984), *Contemporary Feminist Thought*, Unwin, London.

Eisenstein, Z. R. (ed.) (1979), *Capitalist Patriarchy and the Case for Socialist Feminism*, Monthly Review Press, New York.

Ellyard, P. (1981), 'Education and the environment: Where do they meet?', in *Proceedings of the First National Conference of the Australian Association for Environmental Education*, Adelaide, October 1980.

Fensham, P. (1978), 'Stockholm to Tbilisi – the evolution of environmental education', *Prospects* 8(4), 446–55.

Freire, P. (1985), *The Politics of Education: Culture, Power and Liberation*, Bergin & Garvey, Boston, Mass.

Hartsock, N. (1979), 'Feminist theory and the development of revolutionary strategy', in Z. R. Eisenstein (ed.), *Capitalist Patriarchy and the Case for Socialist Feminism*, Monthly Review Press, New York.

Kelly, P. (1984), 'Women and the future', quoted in Cambridge Women's Peace Collective, *My Country is the Whole World: An Anthology of Women's Work on Peace and War*, Pandora Press, London.

Leiss, W. (1972), *The Domination of Nature*, Braziller, New York.

Levene, N. (1986), 'Peace is more than banning bombs', in J. Weston (ed.), *Red and Green: A New Politics of the Environment*, Pluto Press, London.

Millett, K. (1977), *Sexual Politics*, Virago, London.

Mitchell, J. (1971), *Woman's Estate*, Vintage Books, New York.

Monk, J., & Williamson-Fien, J. (1986), 'Stereoscopic visions: Perspectives on gender – challenges for the geography classroom', in J. Fien & R. Gerber (eds), *Teaching Geography for a Better World*, Australian Geography Teachers Association with Jacaranda Press, Brisbane.

Morgan, R. (ed.) (1984), *Sisterhood is Global*, Anchor/Doubleday, New York.

Pepper, D. (1984), *The Roots of Modern Environmentalism*, Croom Helm, London.

Porritt, J. (1984), *Seeing Green*, Blackwell, Oxford.

Porter, P. (1986), *Gender and Education* (EED432 *Sociology of the School*), Deakin University, Vic.

Redclift, M. (1986), 'Redefining the environmental "crisis" in the South', in J. Weston (ed.), *Red and Green: A New Politics of the Environment*, Pluto Press, London.

Robottom, I. M. (1985), Contestation and continuity in educational reform: A critical study of innovations in environmental education, Unpublished PhD thesis, School of Education, Deakin University, Vic.

Rowbotham, S., Segal, L., & Wainwright, H. (1979), *Beyond the Fragments: Feminism and the Making of Socialism*, Merlin Press, London.

Ruether, R. R. (1975), *New Woman New Earth: Sexist Ideologies and Human Liberation*, Seabury Press, New York.

Schumacher, E. F. (1973), *Small is Beautiful: A Study of Economics as if People Mattered*, Blond & Briggs, London.

Spender, D. (1982), *Invisible Women: The Schooling Scandal*, Writers & Readers, London.

Stanley, L., & Wise, S. (1983), *Breaking Out: Feminist Consciousness and Feminist Research*, Routledge & Kegan Paul, London.

Stapp, W. B. (1970), 'The concept of environmental education', *Educational Digest* March, 7–12.

Stone, M. (1976), *When God was a Woman*, Dial Press, New York.

Strange, P. (1983), *It'll Make a Man of You: A Feminist View of the Arms Race*, Peace News/Mushroom, Nottingham.

Tuntawiroon, N. (1986), 'North-South dialogue', in *Proceedings of the North American Association for Environmental Education Conference*, Banff, Alberta.

United Nations Educational, Scientific and Cultural Organization (1980), *Environmental Education in the Light of the Tbilisi Conference*, UNESCO, Paris.

Weston, J. (ed.) (1986), *Red and Green: A New Politics of the Environment*, Pluto Press, London.

Women: A World Report (A New Internationalist Book) (1985), Methuen, London.

Women and Geography Study Group of the Institute of British Geographers (1984), *Geography and Gender: An Introduction to Feminist Geography*, Hutchinson, London.

Women in the World: An International Atlas (1986), Pan, London.

Annotated bibliography

Ruether, R. R. *New Woman New Earth: Sexist Ideologies and Human Liberation.* Seabury Press, New York, 1975.

In this book, Ruether examines the oppressive ideologies and structures supporting sexism and presents an analysis of the socio-economic status of women in modern society. She analyses the interrelationships between sexism, racism and classism through history with specific emphasis on how these social prejudices are ideologically produced and reproduced through religion. One of the major themes running through the book is the way in which patriarchal values of domination and alienation in modern capitalist societies create and sustain sexism (and racism and classism) and therefore provide the ideological justification for ecological destruction. The final chapter looks critically at the social and ecological effects of patriarchal/capitalist history and suggests alternative forms of human and ecological relationships.

Spender, D. *Invisible Women: The Schooling Scandal.* Writers & Readers, London, 1982.

Dale Spender's *Invisible Women* is a study of how the schooling system reinforces and reproduces the oppressive social relations of sexism. The crux of her analysis is a critique of society's notion of 'truth' and of the 'objectivity' of knowledge that forms the basis of what is taught in schools. Her thesis is that under the guise of 'scientific objectivity' the injustice of sexist attitudes, beliefs and practices is perpetuated and justified through the school curriculum. The book charts the history of knowledge generation and the way in which women's contributions have been systematically kept 'off the record' or trivialised. It then discusses aspects of classroom dynamics and shows how boys are socialised to achieve and girls to please. The final chapters of the book document some of the changes in the education system (mainly in Anglo-Western countries) that are challenging the dominance of the white male system and redressing the sex-based disadvantages in schools.

Weston, J. (ed.). *Red and Green: A New Politics of the Environment*. Pluto Press, London, 1986.

The collection of essays presented in this book critically examines the current trends in environmentalism. The authors use a political-economic framework for analysing the fundamental causes of environmental problems and their solutions. Each essay focuses on a specific theme, such as peace, information technology, the inner-city environment or energy, and analyses it through a socialist perspective. All argue, in different ways, that the most basic environmental problem is poverty caused by the economics of profit and loss, seen only in cash terms, of international capitalism. One of the criticisms of modern day 'Green politics' is the narrow definition of 'environment' that is concerned primarily with nature. The authors advocate a 'social environmentalism' and urge the 'greens' to become more 'red'.

Learning with environments: Towards an ecological paradigm for education

Noel Gough

Introduction

THE IDEA OF an ecological paradigm for education is rather abstract, and it might there-fore be best to begin by giving an example of what this idea could mean in practice. Fortunately, Ursula Le Guin (1985) has described in rich and imaginative detail a culture in which education is shaped by an ecological worldview. The Kesh live in a different time and place from us (precisely when and where does not matter for my purposes). What follows is an abridged version of the life story of one of the Kesh, a man called Fairweather; this story, and especially the translator's note which accompanies it, reveals much about the Kesh view of learning.

> He was well educated in his household . . . and became a member of the Planting Lodge at thirteen years old . . . During his adolescence he learned arboriculture with his mother's brother, a scholar of the Planting Lodge . . . and with orchard trees of all kinds.
> . . . he came to Kastoha-na, where he [studied] the way the trees grew there, as the orchards of Kastoha were the richest and most beautiful anywhere in those times . . . Fair-weather . . . went to live in the household of . . . a forester, working mostly with the oaks that are cut for fine carpentry. For some years he worked with her in locating, selecting, cutting, and replanting forest oaks. He joined the Wood Art.
> Whenever he was back in Kastoha he worked at crossbreeding varieties of pear. In those times none of the Valley pears was very good, all were subject to cankers, and most needed irrigation to bear well. To obtain varieties of trees . . . he asked people in the north for help. Some seedling pear trees were sent to him from orchards . . . far in the north . . . By crossbreeding the northern trees with a pear tree he had found growing wild above the oak forests . . . he came upon a strong, small, and drought-hardy tree with excellent fruit, and he came to Sinshan to plant some of the seedlings. Now this is the brown pear grown in most orchards and gardens, and people call it the Fairweather pear . . .
> Fairweather began to study with the apple trees of the Upper Valley orchards, working at crossbreeding to help the mountain apples resist the edge-curl disease. He was also doing a great work of many years with the soils and earths of the foothills of the Mountain and the trees that grew in the various soils, learning where and how they grew . . .
> He continued to work in the orchards of Sinshan, planting, tending, pruning, cleaning, fertilising, weeding, and picking . . . till he was eighty-one. He died of pneumonia after working in the plum orchards of Sinshan in the rain.
> [Fairweather] was my father's father . . . I am writing this for the library . . . so that he may be remembered for a while when pear trees are planted or orchards praised.
>
> *Translator's note*
> *. . . he learned arboriculture with his mother's brother . . . and with orchard trees of all kinds.*
>
> We would be more likely to say that he learned *from* his uncle *about* orchard trees; but this would not be a fair translation of the repeated suffix *oud*, with, together with. To learn *with* an uncle and trees implies that learning is not a transfer of something by someone to someone, but is a relationship. Moreover, the relationship is considered to be reciprocal.

Such a point of view seems at hopeless odds with the distinction of subject and object considered essential to science. Yet it appears that [Fairweather's] genetic experiments or manipulations were technically skilful, and that he was not ignorant of the theories involved, and it is certain that he achieved precisely what he set out to achieve. And the resulting strain of tree was given his name: a type case, in our vocabulary, of Man's control over Nature. This phrase, however, could not be translated into Kesh, which had no word meaning Nature except *she*, being; and anyhow the Kesh saw the Fairweather pear as the result of a collaboration between a man and some pear trees. The difference of attitude is interesting and the absence of capital letters perhaps not entirely trivial. (LeGuin 1985, pp. 273–5)

The Kesh worldview approximates what we would now call 'deep ecology' (Devall & Sessions 1985). Deep ecology cultivates a 'state of being . . . that sustains the widest (and deepest) possible *identification*' of oneself with one's environments (Fox 1986, p. 87). For the Kesh, this sense of identification or 'ecological consciousness' (Devall & Sessions 1985) is so profound that, as explained above, they have no word for 'nature' but, rather, see themselves and nature as part of 'being'. In such a culture, environmental education as we understand it would be unnecessary, since ecologically desirable actions would naturally 'fall out' of this state of being rather than follow from some moral or intellectual imperative (Fox 1986). But in our culture environmental education seems to be necessary because ecological consciousness is not yet widespread. Unfortunately, while most environmental educators would agree that the achievement of some sort of ecological consciousness in learners is the overarching goal of environmental education, there has been little exploration of what it might mean to have a deeply ecological understanding of education itself. Environmental educators have largely been content to see ecology as a *subject matter*—something to be transferred to learners. While it has been recognised that environmental education ought not to be merely education *in* or *about* environments, I am not convinced that the popular slogan of 'education *for* the environment' is much of an improvement. Apart from being somewhat patronising and anthropocentric (who are we to say what is 'good for' the environment, and which environment is '*the* environment', anyway?), this slogan maintains the sorts of distinctions that tend to work against a deeply ecological worldview—distinctions betweeen subject and object, education and environment, learner and teacher. To have a profoundly ecological understanding of education we must shift our attention from the *objects* of environmental education (such as desired states of the environment or changed human attitudes) to *interrelationships*—to the interactions between people and environments that we call 'learning' and to those interactions between people and other people that we call 'teaching'.

In this essay I argue that, to coin a phrase, environmental educators should 'put their educational money where their ecological mouths are'. I show that the existence of an underlying ecological paradigm for education is not just wishful thinking but, rather, that such a worldview is warranted, defensible and practicable. As a foundation for educational inquiry, an ecological paradigm should give us cause for optimism that we might someday learn to live, and live to learn, *with* environments.

Educational paradigms and paradigm shifts

The significance of paradigms in education is illustrated by Figure 1, which compares the foundations of physical architecture with the paradigms of social 'architecture'. Just as buildings rest upon foundations of clay, sand or rock, so our social institutions are built upon paradigms—the understandings of reality, nature and human nature that are taken for granted in our culture (Mochelle 1986).

Figure 1
Comparison between physical architecture and social architecture

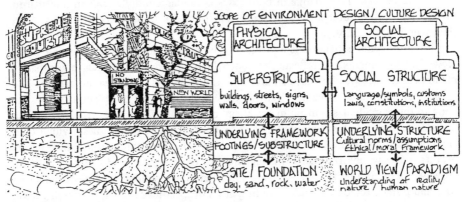

Source: Extract from R. Mochelle, 'Future choice—an environment design approach', *Curriculum Perspectives*, vol. 6, no. 2, 1986, p. 52.

Education is, of course, a piece of social architecture—an institution designed and built by human societies. Much educational reform begins when we notice frictions, failures, faults and flaws in existing structures. Most of the time we do not look too deeply for the causes of such weaknesses—we simply patch up and paint over the cracks in the superstructures of education so as to minimise (at least temporarily) the appearance of weakness. This approach is often ridiculed by calling some reforms 'Band-Aid solutions' or 'additions to an already overcrowded curriculum', but these clichés usually trivialise the reforms in question or ignore the political realities which tend to make educational improvements a matter of evolutionary (rather than revolutionary) change. The plethora of new subject matters which have competed for inclusion in school curricula in recent years—such as environmental education, media studies, computer awareness and peace studies, to name but a few—are quite reasonable educational responses to broader social, technological or environmental changes.

But we cannot always be content with superficial improvements. From time to time we should also investigate the soundness of the underlying structures and paradigms for, if they change or shift, what we build upon them may need to be redesigned and reconstructed, not merely repaired. And it can indeed be argued that our present system of education has been built upon understandings of reality, nature and human nature that can no longer be taken for granted:

> The social construction of reality that once provided a certain coherence to Western society has been unraveling for decades. It was a worldview that valued progress, economic efficiency, science and technology—and saw a world composed of separate entities such as atoms, individuals, academic departments, corporations, cities and nations. (Michael & Anderson 1986, p. 114)

This materialistic and atomistic worldview still dominates formal education, but in human society at large it appears to be under threat. For example, there is some evidence to suggest that there has been a recent strengthening of 'inner-directed' values (ecological, humane, spiritual) in Western industrialised countries, together with a deeper and more subtle shift in beliefs 'away from the confident scientific materialism of the earlier part of this century' (Harman 1985, p. 325). A parallel shift in developing countries is away from Western materialism and towards a reassertion of native cultural values and beliefs. 'The change in both cases is fundamentally a shift in our attitude toward our inner, subjective experience, affirming its importance and its validity' (Harman 1985, p. 325).

Environmental education is a product of both the older and the emerging worldviews and to some extent reflects the contradictions and conflicts that accompany a major paradigm shift. For example, most environmental educators would claim to hold 'ecological' and 'humane' values, but many are also suspicious of 'spiritual' values and cling to the 'confident scientific materialism' of the past. This is particularly evident in formal courses of 'environmental science' or 'environmental studies', which often embody uncritical assumptions about the value of the 'scientific method' in resolving problems of, say, environmental management or the assessment of new technologies. However, if enviromental educators are able to embrace ecological values wholeheartedly and pursue ecological understanding at its deepest levels, then they will be well placed to capitalise on the one feature of the changing worldview that seems most likely to prevail, namely, its *holistic* emphasis:

> The most striking feature of [today's] world is its systemic character, its astounding proliferation of linkages among once-separate cultures, governments, economies and ecosystems . . . everything is connected to everything . . . (Michael & Anderson 1986, p. 115)

Holistic emphases are conspicuous by their absence in most schools – indeed, conventional schools reinforce the view of 'a world composed of separate entities' through every aspect of their design, construction and modes of operation. Age-graded children study separate subjects with specialist teachers in specialised classrooms according to a timetable which both symbolises and brings about a fragmented worldview. One of the very few countervailing tendencies – and one which has been supported by the rhetoric of environmental education – is increasing recognition of the value of 'interdisciplinary' and 'integrated' studies. Such studies are consistent with a shift towards a more holistic worldview but, as will be discussed below, many have done little more than take some forms of ecological understanding as their subject matter.

Ecology as a subject matter

I take 'ecological subject matters' to mean subjects which focus on the interconnections between what were once studied as separate entities. For example, physical science – technology and society (a single subject in Victoria's Higher School Certificate course) allows students to study the ways in which the properties of matter and the workings of machines and human societies are interrelated rather than studying each of them separately in subjects such as chemistry, physics and history. Many of these new subject matters could be described as 'ecological' (and even 'environmental') without necessarily being what is conventionally understood by the term 'environmental education'. For example, the 1970s in Australia saw the birth of both environmental education and media studies as distinctive areas of the school curriculum. Both subjects involve a partial study of human ecology, which *The Concise Oxford Dictionary* defines as a 'study of interaction of persons with their environment'. Environmental education and media studies are similar in that each attempts to increase the learner's awareness and understanding of (and responsible, skilful interaction with) *some* of his or her environments. Conventional environmental education focuses on human interactions with the environment provided by other living systems of the Earth; media studies focus on the environment created by some of humankind's most pervasive inventions, namely, the texts and technologies of the mass media.

But ecological subject matters can be regarded as only a superficial product of a holistic worldview for at least two reasons. First, such studies may preach a holistic perspective but they still tend to be presented as separate entities. Second, most of these new studies have preserved the teaching practices and learning experiences that go with a fragmented worldview. For example, environmental education in schools (regardless of whether it is a separate subject or 'integrated' with other studies) continues to be dominated by the authority of teachers, textbooks and timetables and by the trivial pursuits of memorising information and routinely performing technical tasks. Nevertheless, ecological subject matters may be crude indicators of changes in underlying cultural norms, assumptions and values. These changes are part of the 'deep ecology' of a paradigm shift; they can be seen as products of our pursuit of deeper understandings of the interrelationships among humans and their environments and of the struggle to reconstruct our worldview in the light of such understandings.

For example, some of the most profound insights into deep human ecology have emerged from the feminist critique of human history and culture. Feminist scholarship has helped us to perceive and understand the global and local destructiveness of partriarchy in its myriad forms – in industralism, militarism, the exploitation of developing countries by transnational corporations, and the gross undervaluing of women's work in maintaining families, communities, societies and ecosystems.[1] But we will have achieved very little *for education* if the feminist critique leads merely to, say, school history being changed from a study of men and warfare ('lies about crimes') to a more inclusive study which recognises the roles of women and celebrates peace. A shift towards an ecological paradigm for education does not simply mean more environmental education (or more peace studies, women's studies and so forth) on school timetables. A paradigm shift involves changes in our total worldview, and it may be very difficult for most educators – even for environmental educators who are confident of the depth of their own ecological understanding – to accept that the education system in which they practise, and of which they are themselves products, provides a structured misrepresentation of reality, nature and human nature.

Evolving an ecological paradigm for education

My concept of an ecological paradigm for education has evolved from several different but interrelated sources – and, indeed, it is still evolving as I continue to act and reflect on the commitments such a worldview entails in the course of my own practice as a teacher educator.

The term 'ecological paradigm' is borrowed from Fred Emery (1981) who, like many other writers, uses terms like 'new' and 'emerging' to distinguish an ecological paradigm from the one he calls 'old' and 'traditional'. These terms are a little misleading because the educational paradigm Emery rejects has dominated merely the last two centuries of Western industrial civilisation, and this is a relatively recent period (and limited location) of human history and culture. Terms like 'old', 'new', 'traditional' and 'emerging' identify changing fashions in education and do not reflect deeper continuities or more enduring positions.

I prefer to think of a shift away from an *epistemological* paradigm and use this terminology for two reasons. First, as commonly used in education, 'epistemology' means the study of the origins and method of knowledge, and the core assumptions of Western industrial society's systems of education rest on an epistemology—on a particular set of theories about how humans gain knowledge of themselves and their world. Second, I take 'epistemological' to refer to the *kinds* of knowledge that are valued. The ancient Greek word *episteme* referred to *theoretic* knowledge, and the kinds of knowledge which have dominated Western education are those which have been structured by Western society's dominant form of theorising, namely, positivist empirical science.

Emery's concept of an ecological paradigm for education is based on his synthesis of the results of relatively recent studies in human perception. However, his argument is lengthy and complex, and I will be able to give only a very brief and oversimplified account of it here.

Support for an ecological paradigm comes also from the longer term history of Western education prior to the scientific revolution and, in particular, from the Aristotelian scholastic curriculum which predominated in Europe until the eighteenth century. Within that scholarly tradition, no strong distinction was made between matters of fact and matters of value (Reid 1981), regardless of whether one was studying nature or human nature. The ideal of scientific detachment, or of any attempt to eliminate human values from supposedly 'objective' worldviews, was rightly regarded as absurd. Thus, the recent strengthening of beliefs in the value of inner, subjective experiences may not so much be evidence of a 'new' paradigm but, rather, can be seen as the re-emergence of a deeper continuity in our culture.

Further support for an ecological paradigm is provided by the apparent success of recent innovative practices in education which seem to be consistent with it. I will focus on Earth Education (or what was once known as 'Acclimatisation'). Earth Education is significant not just because it exemplifies good practice in environmental education but also because some of its key principles and practices are characteristic of an ecological paradigm—although this significance is not acknowledged (and, perhaps, not recognised) by most of its creators and supporters.

These three sources of support for an ecological paradigm will now be elaborated.

Ecological theories of perception

Educational practice in Western industrial society has been shaped, to a very large extent, by a particular set of theories about how it is possible for humans to gain knowledge. But if we allow educational practice to be dominated by such theories we should also ask ourselves the question: what if the theories are wrong?

For two hundred years most of our educational practices have been based on the empiricist theories of perception and knowledge that were put forward by several eighteenth-century philosophers, notably Locke, Berkeley and Hume. Their arguments are still reasonable if we are also prepared to accept that the world is as Newton depicted it and that the transfer of information from an object to a viewer obeys Euclid's geometry. According to this view, light reflected from an object to the retina yields only a 'chaotic two-dimensional representation of reality ... any useful knowledge of a three-dimensional world (such as stops one falling off cliffs) would have to come from some sort of intellectual inference' (Emery 1981, pp. 2–3). Locke, Berkeley and Hume 'proved' that in a Newtonian world, based on Euclidean space, individuals could have no sure knowledge of a world outside them – that stimuli could yield no direct and immediate information about a three-dimensional world of solid, persistent objects and causal relations. To cut a long story short, Herbart spelt out what this implied for educational practice, and the Locke-Herbart paradigm was then refined by the work of behaviourist psychologists like Pavlov, Thorndike, Hull and Skinner. Their refinements allowed the paradigm 'to be preserved in the face of Darwinian challenges as to how such incompetent perceptual systems could have had survival value' (Emery 1981, p. 3). Thus, educational practice since the onrush of positivist science has not valued an individual's perceptions as a source of knowledge. It is held that the meaning of perceptions emerges from intellectual processes of analytic abstraction and logical inference (hence the now taken-for-granted separation of *perception* from *cognition*) and that the prime task of education is to distribute the socially validated knowledge that has been so gained. Learning has thus come to be seen as a process of guided induction into bodies of organised propositional knowledge, the workings of formal logic and the skills of textual expression and comprehension.

It should be clear that some of the theoretic foundations of Western industrial society's systems of education have been under threat for some time. In the early part of this century Newton's Euclidean model of the world was displaced by Einstein's (and it can be argued that Einstein's model has now been replaced – or at least refined – by models emerging from quantum physics). It is not an idle question to ask: what if human perceptual organs are geared to Einstein's time–space continuum and not to Euclid's geometry?

A very serious challenge to empiricist theories of perception comes from the work of Fritz Heider (1959) and others whose research questions the assumption that the *meaning* of perceptions (such as the perception of order) can emerge only from intellectual cogitation. Heider's papers (written in Berlin about 1926–30) were not translated into English until 1959, by which time his research had been parallelled (and was later extended) by Gibson (1979). Heider and Gibson demonstrated the plausibility of an *ecological approach to perception*. Their research suggests that the environment has an informational structure at the level of objects and their causal interactions and that human perceptual systems have evolved to detect and extract that information.

Other researchers in human perception have drawn similar conclusions:

> . . . there is ample evidence that the senses are not only genetically preattuned but become more sensitively calibrated to pick up those exigencies of the environment that bear directly on the survival, success and well-being of the perceiver – what has sometimes been called the 'education of attention'. (Shaw & Pittenger 1977, p. 107)

Emery (1981, p. 15) uses a similar phrase, 'education of the senses', to describe the learning process by which our perceptual systems become 'more sensitively calibrated' to the informational structure of our environments.

Empiricist theories of perception have led us to believe that 'real knowledge is locked up in the storehouses of knowledge that are so jealously guarded by a priesthood of scholars and scientists' (Emery 1981, p. 7) and that the best way to gain access to that knowledge is through years of schooling in the disciplines that have been our means of organising the contents of these 'storehouses'. Ecological theories of perception suggest that limitless information is present in our personal, social and physical environments

and that with an 'education of the senses' we can access as much of it as we need: 'It
is an education in *searching* with our own perceptual systems not an education in how
to someday *research* in the accumulated pile of so-called social knowledge' (Emery 1981,
p. 7). Educating our perceptual systems to search our environments is very similar to
what Edward de Bono calls 'generative thinking'. From his work with learners ranging
from five-year-old children to highly literate adults, de Bono concludes that generative
thinking about our environment and our place in it is a matter of perception, of seeing
things in context, not a matter of puzzling over abstractions in our minds: 'The teaching
of thinking is not the teaching of logic but the teaching of perception' (de Bono 1979,
p. 77).

   Ecological theories of perception also suggest new roles for teachers, liberating
them from being, as it were, tour-guides in 'the accumulated piles of so-called social
knowledge'. In an education of the senses, teaching means guiding learners in the many
and various ways of enhancing their capabilities for extracting information from their
environments (Emery 1981). This involves a 'recentring' of teaching from the
teacher–learner relationship to the interrelations between learners and their environments. For many teachers at present, learners' own perceptions of their environments
are very largely a distraction from absorbing theoretic knowledge, and such teachers
insist that their authority and centrality are preserved. Ecological theories of perception suggest that this approach inhibits learning. Indeed, it is teachers who are very
often distracting students from attending to what is before them in their environments.

   The different educational implications that follow from empiricist and ecological
theories of perception are summarised and compared in Table 1.

Table 1
**Comparison of empiricist and ecological theories of perception and their educational
implications**

Empiricist theories of perception	Ecological theories of perception
Suggest that human perceptual systems provide no reliable knowledge of our world, which can only come through *analytical abstraction* and *logical inference*	Suggest that human perceptual systems have evolved to detect informational struc-ture of environment and become more sensitive through *practice in perception*
Socially structured knowledge (largely theoretic and technical)	Individually structured knowledge (practical, personal)
Education as distribution of structured knowledge	Education as searching environments
Teaching as guided access to the store-houses (museums?) of propositional knowledge	Teaching as creating tools, techniques and settings which sustain learners' perceptual work

   Ecological theories of perception are compelling support for an ecological paradigm
for education. However, the political reality is that Heider's and Gibson's conclusions
are unlikely to convince most educators, parents and employers that an epistemological paradigm is a deeply flawed foundation on which to build educational systems and
programs. The existing system of mass education is powerfully supported by entrenched
social interests and élites. On a more pragmatic level, it is difficult to imagine those

of us who have been inducted into the 'priesthood of scholars and scientists' willingly turning our backs on the storehouses of theoretic knowledge with which we are so familiar or encouraging our students to do likewise. Nor should we. But an ecological paradigm puts the storehouses into proper perspective: they are a *part* (but by no means the whole) of the personal, social and physical environments that an education of the senses should help us to *search*.

Historical roots of an ecological paradigm

The conceptual foundations of an ecological paradigm for education are deeper, and may span a longer time frame, than might be suggested by its links to ecological theories of perception.

Prior to the scientific and industrial revolutions, the disciplines of the medieval scholastic curriculum were conceived as *practical arts* rather than as theoretic 'sciences'. That is, the purposes of studying literature, natural history or social history were essentially the same: to help resolve the practical problems faced by humans when their desires fail to match their circumstances. These disciplines focused on the interrelations between human moral purposes and the personal, social and physical environments in which they were seen to be situated. The goal of scholarship in these disciplines was *practical*, that is, 'to perform good works', rather than *theoretic*, that is, to discover or demonstrate some final good or universal truth (McKeon 1977). The goal changed under the influence of the 'scientific method', and many of the humanities were reconceived as social 'sciences'.

The distinction between theoretic, practical and technical modes of operation goes back to Aristotle's writing. As I have argued elsewhere, a revival of interest in a neo-Aristotelian view of a *practical* curriculum strengthens the case for an ecological paradigm by putting it into a longer term historical perspective (Gough 1985). By comparision with a scholarly tradition which spans more than two thousand years, the epistemological paradigm's dominance of education for a mere two centuries seems like a relatively recent aberration.

Learning that is focused on practical problems is more likely to develop ecological consciousness than learning focused on theoretic or technical concerns. Practical problems can be resolved only in the light of complex human–environment interactions, whereas theoretic and technical problems can be solved in relative isolation. Table 2 provides criteria for distinguishing between theoretical, practical and technical problems and gives examples in each category of questions which might arise in programs of environmental education.

If the questions posed in the respective columns of Table 2 are compared with the sorts of questions posed in conventional programs of environmental education, it will be apparent that the emphases in such programs are for the most part theoretic and technical. Shifting the emphasis towards practical problems would be more consistent with an ecological paradigm. Theoretic and technical questions will still arise, but they are more likely to be self-motivated and to be seen in relation to the complex interactions between humans and their environments from which practical questions, problems and issues emerge.

Because many environmental educators have an academic background in the sciences, they may not have done enough to counter the myth that practical problems can be 'solved', as some educators would have it, by 'applying scientific knowledge,

Table 2
Comparison of theoretical, practical and technical problems

Criteria for distinction	Theoretical problems	Practical problems	Technical problems
Subject matter	Concern matters of universal, general, abstract truth	Concern matters of choice, action and judgment in particular times, places and circumstances	Concern matters of skill and technique in producing an embodiment of an idea, image or pattern
Form of solution	Propositional knowledge ('knowing that . . .'); warranted conclusions and generalisations, usually in the form of a description or explanation	Practical judgment ('knowing I/we should . . .'); defensible decisions which can be justified as probably better or worse than alternatives in the circumstances	Skill ('know-how'); productive procedures – effective means to achieving given or desired ends
Source of problem	States of mind: areas of the 'not known' marked out by what is 'known'	States of affairs in relation to ourselves – conditions which we may wish to change	'States of the art' in relation to products or goals; skills, techniques, tools and procedures we wish to be more productive or effective
Method of solving or resolving problem	Controlled by the guiding principle of logical inference (induction and deduction), e.g. the experiment and other forms of planned 'scientific' inquiry	Deliberation leading to a change in the state of affairs or in our desires, e.g. discussion or debate about alternatives	Controlled by the guiding principle of production, e.g. trial and error
Examples of questions	Why do Australians have a relatively high intake of animal protein?	Should Australians reduce their animal protein intake?	How could Australians reduce their animal protein intake?
	How is sunlight energy transformed into chemical energy?	What sort of heating system should I choose for my house?	How can household energy consumption be decreased?
	What factors affect people's perception of environmental qualities?	Would native trees look better here?	How can we propagate native trees?
	Why is Australia's population increasing?	Should I have children?	What techniques are available for population control?
	What is nuclear energy?	Should Australia export uranium?	How can I make my views known?

methods and skills' (Victoria, Minister of Education 1984, p. 19). Practical problems (if they *are* genuinely practical and not merely technical problems or applications of theory) *necessarily* involve subjectivity. Their resolution requires personal knowledge, critical skills and value judgments, not just the 'objective' methods of the sciences and technologies.

It should also be noted that Aristotle's terms for 'practical' can also be translated as 'political'. Environmental educators sometimes stand accused of political naivety (Huckle 1986), and this could in part be due to the gap between their rhetorical claims to be 'practical' and the reality of environmental education programs which emphasise theoretic and technical problems.

The significance of Earth Education

There are several examples of well-developed educational practices which seem to be consistent with an ecological paradigm but which also seem to have arisen more or less independently of each other and of ecological theories of human perception. In addition to de Bono's approaches to the teaching of thinking, referred to above, examples include 'structural arithmetic' and several approaches to reading and writing (Stern & Stern 1971; Gibson & Levin 1975).

Earth Education (formerly known as 'Acclimatisation') is an approach to environmental education which successfully combines the learning of theoretic knowledge with an education of the senses. Earth Education originated in camp nature programs in the United States of America, and, according to one of its founders, Steve Van Matre, it was 'created partially out of frustration with the usual identifying-collecting-dissection-testing approaches to nature' and to help learners 'build a sense of relationship – through both feelings and understandings – with the natural world' (Van Matre 1979, p. 5). Its consistency with an ecological paradigm is indicated by its emphasis on direct sensory experience and on sharpening learners' perceptions of their environments: 'Our aim is to help young people interact more directly with the fascinating array of living things around them' (Van Matre 1979, p. 7).

I have incorporated approaches modelled on Earth Education into a variety of pre-service and in-service teacher education programs focused not only on environmental education but also on such matters as curriculum design and administration, evaluation in education, future studies, and so on. My experience satisfies me that Earth Education techniques, and strategies modelled on those techniques, are effective in developing learners' perceptual skills and conceptual understandings regardless of subject matter. The strategies are as effective at developing learners' skills in perceiving various institutional practices (such as approaches to assessment of pupils' achievements) as they are in developing sensory awareness of biological diversity. However, most attempts to explain the *reasons* for Earth Education's successes (including Van Matre's own description of the 'mechanics of learning' as he understands them) betray the hegemonic power of the epistemological paradigm. For example, many Earth Education techniques are rationalised as though they exemplified the principles of Skinnerian behaviourism. But I would argue that the effectiveness of Earth Education is better explained by its similarities with, say, de Bono's courses in generative thinking. It is particularly significant that both programs are characterised by the imaginative use of *tools*.

De Bono provides tools which deliberately block or hinder the habit of taking a quick sampling of sensory data, making snap judgments about perceptual offerings and retreating into mental abstraction, classification and generalising. De Bono's tools are designed to help learners by blocking easy slips into perceptual error – they are reminders to look again. These tools make learners conscious of habitual processes and help them to sustain the perceptual work that allows them to gain information from their environments – information that cannot be gained from analytical abstraction and logical inference (Emery 1981). ʹ

The tools used to sharpen sensory awareness in Earth Education programs range from such simple devices as blindfolds and mirrors to more elaborate props and gimmicks, including the mental 'tools' of role play, myth and fantasy. But, in each instance of their use, these tools function in much the same way: to sustain perceptual work as distinct from retreating into abstraction. Earth Education also encourages concept building, especially the handful of big ideas which presently summarise our theoretic knowledge of the ecology of living systems (e.g. energy flow, cycles, inter-relationships, change). But these key concepts are treated less as products of analytic abstraction and logical inference and more as further tools for perceiving and searching natural environments.

Conventional schooling fragments and compartmentalises conceptual under-standing. Learners study their world by examining smaller and smaller bits of it in the form of facts, propositions, definitions, generalisations and abstractions. But while conceptual understanding is highly differentiated, sensory awareness is over-generalised:

> The senses . . . are lumped together in one homogenized mass. Kids are encouraged to believe that they should not trust their own perceptions and thus should do little to sharpen their senses. They are told to be objective, to disregard emotions and feelings, and to experi-ment to find the truth. Even when they 'take a look' at a problem, they rarely *see* anything; they merely talk it to death in the classroom. (Van Matre 1978, p. 7)

In Earth Education, this approach is reversed (see Table 3): 'We differentiate in our sensory awareness and generalize in our conceptual understanding. We strive to strengthen individual senses, but opt for the big picture in understanding life (Van Matre 1979, p. 7). Earth Education programs show how learning settings can be created so as to encourage the simultaneous development of a holistic conceptual understanding of ecology and a highly differentiated sensory awareness of environments. Also, teaching in Earth Education is very much the 'recentred' activity referred to previously. The main task of teaching in Earth Education is to contrive the materials and settings and to provide the tools with which learners can search environments with their own per-ceptual systems. The result is that teachers *and* learners tend to 'share and do' rather than 'show and tell'. For all of these reasons, Earth Education seems to be a useful model of how practical bridges can be built between conventional educational prac-tices and those more characteristic of an ecological paradigm.

The simple framework provided in Table 3 can be used to determine the extent to which an educational program or practice is consistent with a shift towards an eco-logical paradigm. For example, my experience as an examiner of Higher School Certi-ficate environmental science in Victoria leads me to conclude that the subject is neither taught nor assessed in a particularly 'ecological' way. The Earth Education model suggests that the minutiae of the environments being studied are not of foremost import-ance. In environmental science there would seem to be little point in, say, dissecting a frog merely to make a labelled drawing of its digestive system (or whatever). The important conceptual understandings of the subject are ecosystemic and, therefore, are

Table 3
Comparison of conventional schooling and Earth Education

	Concepts	Senses
Conventional schooling (Epistemological)	Differentiated (focus on smaller and smaller bits of material)	Undifferentiated (emphasise thinking more than perceiving)
Earth Education (More ecological)	Undifferentiated (emphasise the big picture)	Differentiated (focus on sharpening individual senses)

Source: Adapted from S. Van Matre, *Sunship Earth: An Acclimatization Program for Outdoor Learning*, American Camping Association, Martinsville, Ind., 1979, p. 8.

concerned more with frogs in relation to ponds and streams, and ponds and streams in relation to water cycles. This is not to say that detail is unimportant in developing ecological understanding but, rather, that the pursuit of detail should be purposeful rather than arbitrary and should follow rather than precede the learner's grasp of the big picture. Thus, concern about the effects of industrial waste discharged into inland waterways might well lead to dissecting a frog to look for evidence of the biological magnification of toxic chemicals.

If one is attempting to assess learners' understandings of the big picture then it follows that an external examination of an ecological study should not require students to recall trivia, minutiae or isolated 'facts', but should provide them with opportunities to demonstrate their perceptual discrimination and conceptual understanding.

Unfortunately, course descriptions for subjects like environmental science are usually written in terms of numerous specific objectives to be mastered and specific items of content to be remembered and comprehended. It would be more consistent with a shift towards an ecological paradigm to provide very broad learning goals and to describe content in terms of key concepts and generalisations which, in turn, could be used as foci for exploration rather than as objects of mastery. In a truly ecological study it should be well nigh impossible for an examiner to write a trivial question requiring nothing more than the recall of factual information.

In helping teachers to adopt an ecological approach, I have found Garth Boomer's idea of teaching as a kind of 'bushcraft' a useful and appropriate metaphor:

> In the ecology of the school 'bush' there is a bewildering array of texts, tests, assignments and artefacts. The teacher should be used to finding interesting and pertinent specimens and talking about their characteristics, habits and habitats. Students should be encouraged to familiarise themselves with funny creatures like science textbooks, learning how to tame them, remembering where dangers lurk and noting little peculiarities.
>
> Teachers should not drive students in a tourist bus through the school curriculum, encouraging the bland recital of tourist blurbs. Students should be obliged to savour the texture of life, wild and rich. (Boomer 1982, p. 119)

The similarities between this view of the school 'bush' and an ecological approach to environmental education should be apparent. The 'bush' of environmental education has its own bewildering array of concepts, conventions, experiences, symbols, slogans, methods, media, techniques and problems. But the 'bush' of environmental education does not only include tangible 'specimens' like frogs, ponds and biomagnified chemicals; it also includes a great deal of territory that exists chiefly in human minds – ideas, plans, perceptions, policies, motivations and interests. When we document courses in environmental education we should try to make them *guides* to such complex environments. They should be seen as *one* way of conceptualising the big picture of environmental education by providing a word map of the territory and a scheme for identifying and, more importantly, *exploring* the interactions among the 'interesting specimens' that can be found in it. Students as well as teachers should be able to 'read' this map and use this scheme – they should be able to use key concepts and generalisations as tools in their own explorations of human–environment interactions.

'Bushcraft' is learned from personal experience and by apprenticeship to someone who models it, such as a teacher who communicates with genuine enthusiasm and flair the perceptual discriminations and conceptual understandings that underlie his or her craft. The key concepts and generalisations of ecological understanding do not occur 'naturally' in environments, examination papers or textbooks, and learners may need assistance to see these human inventions in the real world of human interactions with environments. The 'habitats' of concepts and generalisations are found not only in the natural and built environments but also in various forms of print, visual and electronic media and in everyday discourse. Students should be encouraged to become more adept as connoisseurs and critics of the environment-related *meanings* that abound in popular culture and media. Television programs and commercials, daily newspapers, magazines, and so on, provide numerous examples and illustrations of ecological concepts and generalisations. Indeed, the profusion of environmental concepts, generalisations, problems and issues that can be found in the real worlds of·nature, art, artifice and popular media makes conventional school textbooks almost redundant.

The majority of school textbooks are products of an approach to learning which fragments, compartmentalises and predigests conceptual understanding in a way which is anything but ecological. Most textbooks are dry and dusty museums of ideas and information and encourage 'the bland recital of tourist blurbs'. Textbooks are, indeed, 'funny creatures' and, apart from their occasional use for reference purposes, may do more harm than good if relied upon to excess. Certainly, teachers should familiarise themselves and their students with the 'little peculiarities' of school texts and point out where 'dangers lurk' in their use. For example, many textbooks seriously distort their subject matter in some way. I have lost count of the number of science textbooks (and teachers, for that matter) that persistently misuse, and distort the meaning of, the term 'experiment'. The 'experiments' which science textbooks encourage students to conduct are nearly always *demonstrations* of theoretic knowledge or a technical procedure. They are usually designed to *show* something to students and rarely encourage genuine inquiry. Yet experimentation is among the most fundamental procedures of the scientific method. Distortion of the concept in textbooks erodes the uncritical reader's understanding of the very methods these texts purport to encourage.

Educational practices which support learning with environments

The educational practices and experiences which characterise epistemological and ecological paradigms are summarised and compared in Table 4. It will be apparent that

Table 4
Summary of differences between epistemological and ecological paradigms of education

	Epistemological	Ecological
The practice		
Object of learning	Transmission of existing knowledge Abstraction of generic concepts	Perception of invariants Discovery of serial concepts Discovery of universals in particulars *in learners' environments*
Control of learning	Asymmetrical dependence Teacher–pupil Competition between learners	Symmetrical dependence Co-learners Co-operation between learners
Co-ordination of learning (a) behaviour settings (b) timing	Schools/classrooms Age-grading school calendar and class timetable	Community settings Synchronised to and negotiated with community settings
Learning materials	Textbooks Standardised procedures (e.g. lab. exercises)	Reality-centred projects
Learning activity	Paying attention Rote activities Memorising	Discrimination Differentiation Searching Creating
Teaching activity	Lecturing Demonstrating	Creating and re-creating learning settings
System principle	Pedagoguery	Discovery
The experience		
Cultural mode	Work/religion 'Serious drudgery'	Active leisure 'Exciting, frustrating'
Dominant group emotions	Dependency Fight–flight	Pairing
Personal development	Conformity–bullying Divorce of means and ends–cheating Self-centredness (autonomy) Hatred of learning (and swots)	Tolerance of individuality Depth and integration Equal consideration of self and others (homonomy) Learning as living

Source: Adapted from F. Emery, 'Educational paradigm', *Human Futures*, Spring, 1981, p. 15.

many of the practices and experiences listed under 'ecological' are supported by much of the rhetoric of educational reform in Australia during the past two decades. Moves towards more school-based curriculum development, greater community involvement in school decision making, increasingly non-competitive and co-operative assessment practices, more issues-based and inquiry-based learning, and so on, all seem to be consistent with an ecological paradigm for education. However, this consistency may be more apparent than real, since each of these reforms may affect practices and procedures in a superficial way without altering underlying purposes and values.

As already noted, the core of Western industrial society's educational worldview lies in assumptions about how people gain *theoretic* knowledge. Many educators who pay lip-service to the practices and experiences which exemplify an ecological paradigm, and many of those who attempt to make such practices and experiences a reality in schools, have not abandoned these underlying assumptions. Thus, they fail to achieve any real change in the objects of learning and the disposition of the learner, because they are still orienting themselves and their learners towards the 'storehouses' of theoretic knowledge. That is, practices which appear to be consistent with an ecological paradigm can be used simply to provide a more attractive route to achieving the objects of an epistemological paradigm. The incorporation of 'reality-centred projects', 'community settings' and the 'co-operation of learners' into many educational programs does not necessarily serve an 'education of the senses' but, rather, may merely make the transmission of existing theoretic knowledge seem more palatable.

But some reformers try to practise what they preach, and it is worth noting that the exemplary programs referred to here seem to be independent outcomes of practical deliberation and judgment – that is, independent *searches* of educational environments – rather than applications of the theoretic foundations of an ecological paradigm. For example, neither de Bono nor Van Matre appears to be aware of Heider (or, for that matter, of each other), and all appear to have created their programs out of their own perceptions and subjective responses to their experiences of alternative practices. Thus, Van Matre states that Earth Education was created partly out of frustration with conventional approaches to environmental education but also, and more importantly,

> it was molded by people who were excited about kids and learning and life itself, who liked to laugh, but who took their work seriously, who wanted to open up new doors of perception for their learners. (Van Matre 1979, p. 5)

Such observations contain implicit challenges for environmental educators. How *should* we open up new doors of perception for our learners and for ourselves? Rethinking all of education – not just environmental education – according to an ecological worldview may seem to be idealistic, but this should not deter us from taking some of the small yet significant steps which might improve our own practices immediately. First, we can try to trust our personal subjective experiences rather than defer habitually to the entrenched status of accumulated propositional knowledge. Second, we can try to educate our own senses so that we become better at searching out the characteristics of the personal, social and physical environments in which we conduct our educational practices. Above all, we can try to see such searching – like all learning – as a relationship. Fairweather, it will be recalled, did not learn *from* an uncle *about* trees, and we should perhaps put less faith in what it is possible to learn *from* lecturers or textbooks *about* children or schools. Rather, like Fairweather, we should have more faith in what we can learn *with* our peers, *with* those we now call our learners, and *with* environments.

Notes

1 See Giovanna Di Chiro's essay in this book.

References

de Bono, E. (1979), *Learning to Think*, Penguin, Harmondsworth.

Boomer, G. (ed.) (1982), *Negotiating the Curriculum: A Teacher–Student Partnership*, Ashton Scholastic, Sydney.

Devall, B., & Sessions, G. (1985), *Deep Ecology: Living as if Nature Mattered*, Gibbs M. Smith, Layton, UT.

Emery, F. (1981), 'Educational paradigms', *Human Futures*, Spring, 1–17.

Fox, W. (1986), *Approaching Deep Ecology: A Response to Richard Sylvan's Critique of Deep Ecology* (Environmental Studies Occasional Paper no.20), Board of Environmental Studies, University of Tasmania, Hobart.

Gibson, E., & Levin, H. (1975), *The Psychology of Reading*, MIT Press, Cambridge, Mass.

Gibson, J.J. (1979), *The Ecological Approach to Visual Perception*, Houghton Mifflin, Boston, Mass.

Gough, N. (1985), *Curriculum Programs for Practical Learning*, Curriculum Branch, Education Department of Victoria, Melbourne.

Harman, W.W. (1985), 'Colour the future green?: The uncertain significance of global green politics', *Futures* **17**(4), 318–30.

Heider, F. (1959), *On Perception and Event Structure and the Psychological Environment: Select Papers*, International Universities Press, New York.

Huckle, J. (1986), 'Ten red questions to ask green teachers', *Green Teacher* **1**(2), 11–15.

Le Guin, U. (1985), *Always Coming Home*, Harper & Row, New York.

McKeon, R. (1977), 'Person and community: Metaphysical and political', *Ethics* **88**(3), 207–17.

Michael, D.N., & Anderson, W.T. (1986), 'Norms in conflict and confusion', in H. F. Didsbury, Jr (ed.), *Challenges and Opportunities: From Now to 2001*, World Future Society, Bethesda, Md.

Mochelle, R. (1986), 'Future choice—an environment design approach', *Curriculum Perspectives*, **6**(2), 52.

Reid, W.A. (1981), 'The deliberative approach to the study of the curriculum and its relation to critical pluralism', in M. Lawn & L. Barton, (eds), *Rethinking Curriculum Studies*, Croom Helm, London.

Shaw, R., & Pittenger, J. (1977), 'Perceiving the face of change in changing faces', in R. Shaw & J. Bransford, *Perceiving Action and Knowing: Toward an Ecological Psychology*, Wiley, New York.

Stern, C., & Stern, M. (1971), *Children Discover Arithmetic*, Harper & Row, New York.

Van Matre, S. (1979), *Sunship Earth: An Acclimatization Program for Outdoor Learning*, American Camping Association, Martinsville, Ind.

Victoria, Minister of Education (1984), *Curriculum Development and Planning in Victoria* (Ministerial Paper no.6) Education Department of Victoria, Melbourne.

Annotated bibliography

Lawn, M., & Barton, L. (eds). *Rethinking Curriculum Studies*. Croom Helm, London, 1981.

Most writers in the literature of curriculum studies make suggestions about courses of action or describe conceptual frameworks which purport to be 'practical' in their applicability to schools and classrooms. But a major difficulty with this literature is that many of these same writers tend to disguise or avoid discussion of their own ideological and intellectual assumptions and presuppositions. One of the great strengths of *Rethinking Curriculum Studies* is that the majority of its contributing authors seem to be acutely aware of this difficulty and do their best to reveal their own and others' worldviews. As its title suggests, the book critically reappraises curriculum studies and offers a variety of alternative ways of perceiving, clarifying, exploring and resolving the persistent practical problems of curriculum work. The contributions are diverse, but they embody a shared view of curriculum work as an activity which is inherently problematic, political and susceptible to improvement through participatory inquiry and practical deliberation. None of the authors addresses environmental education as such, but all provide insights which are pertinent to the development of environmental education curricula. The chapters by William Reid and Madeleine Grumet are particularly insightful in their different but complementary ways and deserve the close attention of anyone with an interest in curriculum improvement and the reconstruction of curriculum studies.

Le Guin, U. *Always Coming Home*. Harper & Row, New York, 1985.

Speculative fiction, including that which is popularly known as science fiction, is an important resource for environmental education. Most science fiction deals with the changed relationships between humans and environments that might be wrought by developments in science and technology. Much science fiction also brings vividly to life, and critically evaluates, some of the cherished myths of Western culture, including the assumed beneficence of science and technology and the view of the Earth as a resource for human exploitation. *Always Coming Home* is speculative fiction at its very best. It is set some 2600 years hence, in an imagined version of California's Napa Valley. It is not a novel in the conventional sense. Rather, it consists chiefly of the voices of the valley's people speaking for themselves in stories, life stories, histories, poetry, songs, plays, ceremonies, medical practices, recipes, and so on (the book is illustrated and a cassette tape of music and poetry is available with it). Thus, Le Guin gives the reader clues, bits and hints – an archeology of a future culture in which industrial technologies have faded. The valley is by no means a Utopia, but by the standards of Western industrial society the valley dwellers have a deeply ecological worldview. Le Guin's particular genius is that she not only describes this worldview by reference to abstractions (such as the cosmology of the valley people), but also provides concrete examples of this ecological worldview as it is manifested in art, craft, commerce and culture. For environmental educators, the particular significance of *Always Coming Home* is that it provides a rich and compelling vision of what it might mean to learn to live – and live to learn –*with* environments.

Van Matre, S. *Sunship Earth: An Acclimatization Program for Outdoor Learning*. American Camping Association, Martinsville, Ind., 1979; also, from the same author and publisher, *Acclimatization* (1972), *Acclimatizating* (1974) and (with Kirk Hoessle) *Earth Magic* (1980) and *Snow Walks* (1980).

Steve Van Matre coined the term 'Acclimatization' during the 1960s to describe activities and programs designed to help children (and, later, people of all ages) build a sense of relationship with the natural world. The evolution of Acclimatization as a coherent philosophy and a style of practice in environmental education can be traced in the series of highly readable books and activity manuals cited above. The introductory section of *Sunship Earth* (pp. xv–30) is a particularly useful summary of the distinguishing features of Acclimatization and provides a rationale for its main elements. These elements are sharpening the senses, building key ecological concepts, providing opportunities for solitude, providing structured learning experiences, and making learning a joyful and 'magical' experience. In 1984 Acclimatization was renamed 'Earth Education'. The Institute for Earth Education (IEE) now operates as a non-profit, volunteer, worldwide network. The IEE is active in Australia, and there is a strong demand from many school and community groups for its programs and resources, and for the services of its associates. Earth Education programs and activities, with their ingenious uses of props, gimmicks and novelty, offer inspirational alternatives to the kinds of activities (such as identifying, naming, collecting and dissecting) which may have become stereotypical in environmental education.

Schooling and environmental education: Contradictions in purpose and practice

Robert B. Stevenson

Introduction[1]

A NUMBER OF authors have observed a pronounced discrepancy between the problem-solving and action-oriented goals associated with the contemporary philosophy of environmental education and an emphasis on the acquisition of environmental knowledge and awareness in school programs (Childress 1978; Greenall 1981; Maher 1982; Robottom 1982; Volk, Hungerford & Tomera 1984). Content analyses have revealed that curriculum materials commonly used for environmental education in Australia and the United States of America deviate from the rhetoric in a similar way (Robottom 1983; Stevenson 1984).

In this essay I argue that this rhetoric–reality gap is to be expected given the traditional purpose and structure of schooling. A discussion of its historical development sets the contemporary concept of environmental education in the context of the political activism of the environmental movement. The socially critical and political action goals of environmental education are contrasted, first, with nature study and conservation education, and then with the uncritical role of schooling in maintaining the present social order. The need for students to engage in ideological and critical inquiry is indicated by an examination of the different ideologies which underlie proposals for environmental reform. Such educational ideals, however, conflict with the dominant practices in schools, which emphasise the passive assimilation and reproduction of simplistic factual knowledge and an unproblematic 'truth'. These practices are then explained by examining the structural organisation of schools, the primacy of demands on teachers to maintain order and control, and teachers' presuppositions about knowledge and teaching.

The historical context of the development of environmental education

The origins of environmental education can be traced, first, to the promotion of nature and outdoor study, essentially in primary schools, and later to the conservation movement. Nature study gained prominence through the school camps movement in Australia (Reid 1980; Strom 1980), rural studies in Britain (Wheeler 1975) and the publication of Wilbur Jackman's *Nature Study for the Common Schools* in the United States of America in 1891 (Stapp 1974). The primary purpose of nature study was – and still is – to develop an understanding and appreciation of the natural environment through first-hand observations. The conservation movement, which grew gradually during the first half of this century, introduced a concern for the preservation of species and areas of natural significance through sound management. This concern was expressed in moral and aesthetic terms by Aldo Leopold in *A Sand County Almanac* (1948) and in political (albeit conservative) terms by the formation of the International Union for the Conservation of Nature and Natural Resources. Historically, conservation education has concentrated on helping 'the public better understand the importance of natural resources to our society, and [developing] citizen support for natural resource management programs' (Stapp 1974, p. 46).

Both of these movements were rooted in the liberal-progressive educational philosophies of, for example, Dewey, Rugg and Counts (Robottom 1985) and had modest educational and environmental goals. Their social and political character reflected the middle class and the liberal democratic tradition that dominates Western capitalist societies. In other words, neither nature study nor conservation education challenged the socio-economic or political fabric of our society. Reviews of school practices generally indicated that nature study's and conservation education's aims of developing knowledge, skills and awareness about natural resources and their management were fairly widely incorporated into primary school curricula and the science and geography curricula of secondary schools (Childress 1978; United Nations Educational, Scientific and Cultural Organization 1977).

Beginning with Rachel Carson's *Silent Spring* (1962), the 1960s brought warnings of imminent ecological disasters. Extensive media coverage of environmental issues, the publication of numerous books by ecologists, and the emergence of organisations such as Friends of the Earth and Zero Population Growth reflected a widespread concern in the late 1960s and early 1970s that action was needed to change the prevailing pattern of misuse of the environment.

Originally, this concern was part of a broader grass-roots movement which was centred on a desire for a lifestyle that emphasised the expression of both individuality and community (as a reaction against conformity and isolation), and a quality of life based on non-materialistic values. The issues of civil rights (in the United States of America), student rights and military imperialism, as well as environmental exploitation, became the focus of a dramatic increase in political activism (in both sanctioned and disapprobated forms) by a significant minority of citizens throughout much of the industrialised Western world.

Although part of the social consciousness of this period reflected a concern for the disadvantaged status of racial and class minorities, the environmental movement throughout the Western world was criticised as 'the revolt of the *élite* and well-informed middle classes' who ignored the problems of the urban environment in which the majority of people lived (Wheeler 1975, p. 14). In Australia and Britain, however, the working class did become involved to some extent, as a result of the impact on their lives of planning decisions intended to 'improve' the built environment (Wheeler 1975). 'Green bans' on so-called urban renewal projects were instigated in Australia by trade unions, and bitter conflicts erupted in both countries over issues concerning places of considerably lower status than wilderness areas or historic buildings. Thus, for the first time the environmental movement expanded across class boundaries (at least in these two countries) and broadened understanding of the term 'environment' to include urban (or built), social, economic and political aspects as well as natural, historic and aesthetic elements.

Governments and institutions responded to these community concerns by, for example, establishing new government agencies with responsibility for monitoring and regulating the environmental impact of industry, inviting community participation in urban planning, and introducing university courses and departments in environmental management. At the international level the response included the involvement of the United Nations in developing a program of action (e.g. conferences, reports, policy statements) to determine and promote the role of education in environmental improvement. In this context a third and more radical phase of development, now termed 'environmental education', evolved with a new philosophy which embodied a commitment to activism.

Ideological conflicts within the environmental movement

While there was consensus within the environmental movement concerning the symptoms of environmental degradation, the underlying causes and the means of averting further catastrophe were – and remain – in dispute even among professional ecologists. Major blame has been attributed variously to population growth, modern industrial technology, the capitalist economic system, economic growth and an affluent consumer society in which materialistic values predominate (Attfield 1983). As revealed by the debate between representatives of industrial and developing countries at the 1972 United Nations Conference on the Human Environment in Stockholm, explanations of and proposed solutions to our environmental problems can represent ideologies which have particular social and political agendas. For example, countries which do not wish to disturb their current pattern of resource use are seeking to maintain (either consciously or unconsciously) the existing social and economic order. On the other hand, developing countries arguing for a more equitable distribution of resources want to transform the present arrangement of global economic and political power.

A number of typologies (for example, Devall & Sessions 1985; Enzensberger 1974; Fox 1984; Huckle 1983) have been constructed to illuminate the ideologies underlying different visions of and means to environmental improvement. Although these typologies often distinguish different emphases on a number of dimensions, one common and critical dimension is the political scenario through which environmental reform is to be enacted. Essentially, one of two broad scenarios is embraced (if not explicitly, at least implicitly) with two variations on the type of approach adopted within each[2]:

1 Conservative reform (within the present system)
   (a) The *technical approach* is concerned with developing 'quick technological fixes' of environmental conflicts (Enzensberger 1974) by injecting ecological principles and information into existing decision-making structures. Its adherents believe that scientific and technological expertise can provide the basis for resolving quality-of-life issues without the need for social and economic changes (O'Riordan 1981). In this approach there is no place for non-professional or citizen participation in environmental planning
   (b) The *political approach* involves working within the present political system to reduce the impact of human activity on the environment. These reformers foresee a need for improving legal, political, economic and technological decision making, but without addressing the structure of our social and economic institutions. Typical concerns are the preservation of open space and wilderness areas and the siting of undesirable development projects (such as airports, freeways and factories): in other words, issues that impinge on the quality of life of the middle class who have the clout to use the conventional political process effectively.

Both the technical and the political approaches, partly by supporting the primacy of economic growth, tend to maintain the status quo rather than transform the economic and political order.

2   Radical reform (of the present system)
   (a) The *socially critical approach* treats environmental crises as symptoms of a larger problem in our society (Huckle 1983), namely the dominant role of economic considerations and the unequal distribution of resources. Radical reformers regard major economic reorganisation as the only way to rectify violations of both environmental quality and social justice. Most Marxists and neo-Marxists attribute the problem to capitalism (i.e. private ownership of the mode of production), while others point out the equally serious nature of environmental destruction in socialist countries (Enzensberger 1974). Disagreement on the means of reform tends to be accompanied by the lack of a clear vision of an alternative economic and political system.
   (b) The *alternative approach* rejects traditional forms of society and advocates a virtually pre-industrial lifestyle involving a closer relationship with nature in small, self-sufficient (usually rural) communities. This Utopian alternative, which is presently feasible for very few people, includes reliance on soft or low-impact technologies. 'Deep' ecologists or environmentalists, who emphasise the intrinsic (rather than instrumental) value of all of nature, often are included in this category (Huckle 1983). However, many deep ecologists combine the cultivation of a personal environmental ethic with political activism by addressing public policy through the vehicle of the Green Party (Devall & Sessions 1985). In this latter respect they have more in common with the socially critical reformers, but with less concern for social inequalities.

Both socially critical and alternative reformers argue that economic growth should be a subsidiary consideration to environmental quality. However, socially critical environmentalists see the alternative group as politically naive and retreatist since 'their idealism meets the socio-psychological needs of a disillusioned middle class whose environment is threatened for the first time in history, but is largely irrelevant to the vast majority which has far more pressing concerns' (Huckle 1983, p. 103).

Contemporary goals of environmental education

The different ideologies associated with the environmental movement have two important implications for education. By revealing the existence of substantively different perspectives of the root causes of environmental problems and of the appropriate means to effecting change, the implication is that students should examine all perspectives and judge their respective merits. Several writers (Huckle 1983; Maher 1986), in contending that only (what I have termed) the socially critical approach to radical reform is consistent with the goals and principles of contemporary environmental education, have implied that teachers and students should be concerned with this ideological position only. I would argue that to be consistent with democratic principles students should be exposed to the plurality of environmental ideologies, and that through a process of inquiry, critique and reflection they can be assisted to develop and defend their own set of environmental beliefs and values. After engaging in this rational process of social inquiry and moral deliberation, it should be each student's choice to pursue actions deemed necessary and justifiable for achieving environmental reform in accordance with the ideological position he or she supports. But students also need to be competent to implement or act on their choice, otherwise they will not consider themselves capable of rectifying environmental injustices, and therefore will not experience an authentic choice on these issues (Newmann 1975). In other words, without the ability to act on their choice, they in effect have no choice.

The development of this competence leads to the second implication. The ideologies illustrate that environmental reform is political (no position is politically or socially neutral). Therefore, if students are to be capable of acting on their choices and influencing environmental decision making, then environmental education must incorporate the development of students' knowledge of the political-legal process and skills in political advocacy. As well as examining the formal and informal processes of decision making in the political-legal system, students should be encouraged to analyse the various forms of political participation so that they can rationally justify the strategies for action which will employ their advocacy skills (Newmann, Bertocci & Landsness 1977).

These implications are consistent with the environmental education process, as enunciated in the contemporary rhetoric. The goals of environmental education include the intellectual tasks of critical appraisal of environmental (and political) situations and the formulation of a moral code concerning such issues, as well as the development of a commitment to act on one's values by providing opportunities to participate actively in environmental improvement. The influential and widely accepted policy statements that emerged from the international conferences at Belgrade in 1975 and Tbilisi in 1977 established a clear consensus on this point. For example, in addition to prescribing the development of critical thinking and problem-solving and decision-making skills in the context of quality-of-life issues, the Tbilisi Declaration emphasised that students should 'be actively involved at all levels in working toward resolution of environmental problems' (Tbilisi Declaration 1978, p. 18).

While the goals of nature study and conservation education could be relatively easily accommodated in the goals and structural organisation of schools, this more recent critical and action orientation of environmental education creates a far more challenging task for schools. To assess the nature, extent and causes of this challenge we need to examine the purpose and practice of schooling.

The social and cultural purpose of schooling

Schools as we know them today evolved in the early nineteenth century as institutions for mass education. Their intended purpose, according to Dewey, was to transmit basic knowledge and the skills of reading, writing and arithmetic, as well as to convey a broad understanding of society and the student's role in it (Schrag, in press). In other words, schools, and hence classrooms, were structured to present basic information, to enable the practice of routine skills, and to maintain existing social conditions and relations. Given the universality and stability of their structural organisation over almost two centuries, it seems that schools in the form of classrooms generally are efficient in meeting the above purpose (Schrag, in press).

Historically then, schools were not intended to develop critical thinkers, social inquirers and problem solvers, or active participants in environmental and political (or even educational) decision making. Put simply, their intended function was not to promote social change or reconstruction.

Educational sociologists have described the contemporary role of schools as still primarily concerned with the transmission of cultural knowledge, skills and values. But modern industrialised societies, with their specialised division of labour creating social stratification, contain a plurality of cultures and subcultures, each of which possesses unique knowledge and values. Therefore, compulsory public schooling is faced with choices in defining the culture it is to transmit. These choices ultimately reflect the 'mainstream' or dominant beliefs, values and norms shared by those who have political power in our society (Apple 1979; Lundgren 1981; Popkewitz 1983). And one of the dominant beliefs is that the role of schools should include credentialling students with respect to their ability to demonstrate mastery of 'valued' knowledge and skills. Students' assessed performance then becomes a significant determinant of their life chances and economic well-being. The well-known consequence of this credentialling role is that the participants see the 'real' purpose of schooling as the pursuit of individual academic achievements. Schools thereby convey norms of individualism, competition, achievement and independence: norms that prevail in the dominant culture and maintain the existing structure of society. Hence, as Durkheim (1956) argued, one role of schooling is to foster and perpetuate social stability. In this respect, schooling also contributes, along with other social institutions, to the reproduction of social and economic inequalities (on the basis of class, race and gender) in society, since some groups have less experience of and more limited access to culturally valued forms of knowledge (Apple 1982).

The rhetoric of environmental education, on the other hand, focuses on improving the quality of life of all humankind on our planet by finding 'ways to ensure that no nation should grow or develop at the expense of another nation and that the consumption of no individual should be increased at the expense of other individuals' (Belgrade Charter in Fensham 1976, p. 24). Several key aspirations are embedded in this statement. First, environmental education is concerned not only with social reconstruction to alleviate exploitation of the environment, but also with the avoidance of social injustices in the process of that reconstruction. Second, ecological harmony and social justice suggest the need for an interdependent community (at both global and local levels), rather than the liberal, capitalist notion of a community of free or autonomous individuals without collective responsibility (which may demand forgoing certain individual interests). Invariably, both tasks undermine social stability by creating conflict, since they challenge dominant interests and different value systems.

Contemporary environmental education, therefore, has the revolutionary purpose of transforming the values that underlie our decision making, from the present ones which aid and abet environmental (and human) degradation to those which support a sustainable planet in which all people live with equal human dignity (Tanner 1974). This contrasts with the traditional purpose of schools, as described above, of conserving the existing social order by reproducing the norms and values that currently dominate environmental decision making. Therein lies the first major contradiction between environmental education and schooling.

Curriculum and pedagogical practices
The guiding principles (Tbilisi Declaration 1978) and key characteristics (Fensham 1979) of environmental education establish particular kinds of curriculum and pedagogical practices as being necessary to achieve the stated goals. They focus on learners

working individually and collectively towards the resolution of current environmental problems. The particular problems should, of course, be appropriate to students' cognitive and experiential development and can range from small-scale, local concerns (e.g. trail bike use in a wildlife reserve) to major global issues (e.g. desertification). Teaching and learning are intended to be co-operative processes of inquiry into and action on real environmental issues. Such an inquiry process demands that students actively engage in critical or complex thinking about real problems. The development of knowledge, skills and values is not only directed towards action, but emerges in the context of preparing for (i.e. the inquiry) and taking action. Consequently, curriculum and pedagogical planning need to be highly flexible. For example, as well as adapting to students' own social constructs, the teacher should be amenable to students' decisions in relation to both their learning and their actions.

In contrast, numerous studies have indicated that there is one consistent, and markedly different, pattern to the curriculum and pedagogical practices to be found in the majority of classrooms (e.g. Barnes 1969, 1976; Bellack et al. 1966; Cusick 1977; Everhart 1983; Goodlad 1984; Sizer 1984). The common curriculum emphasis can be described as the mastery of many fragmented facts, concepts and simple generalisations organised loosely within discrete bodies or fields of study. The predominant pedagogical process involves the teacher as dispenser of factual knowledge. Official student participation is usually limited to making short oral (or, less frequently, written) responses to teacher questions which elicit 'largely recitation of information already defined by the teacher or textbook' (Young 1980, p. 68). The teacher is frequently the only participant who actively engages in higher order thinking processes, such as the critical analysis of explanations and arguments and the making of value judgments. Characteristically, student thinking is confined to applying factual information to familiar 'well-structured' problems: that is, problems with unambiguous definitions and goals, and a single correct solution which has already been determined (Simon 1973). Beyond such relatively simple application, knowledge is acquired individually for future use (i.e. in later life). The test of students' thinking occurs in private artificial situations (i.e. written examinations) on theoretical material which is usually far removed from the realm of the students' present or future life experiences.

These contrasting practices suggest an extensive list of curriculum and pedagogical contradictions between environmental education and schooling. While an environmental education curriculum should be interdisciplinary and focus on real practical problems, school curricula are discipline-based and emphasise abstract theoretical problems. Whereas a curriculum in environmental education is emergent and problematic in that the content arises as students are involved in specific environmental problems, most school curricula are predefined since they are designed to serve predetermined behaviourally specific ends (that is, ends whose attainment can be readily assessed). Similarly, pedagogy in environmental education ought to be problematic in the sense that the way for students (and teachers) to solve environmental problems is uncertain, in contrast to the unproblematic pedagogy of information dissemination which results from instructional means being clearly defined by the criterion of the efficient achievement of the desired ends (Kliebard 1977). A function of knowledge in environmental education is immediate use for the social value of a sustainable and emancipated quality of life, which conflicts with the major function of school knowledge as storage for future use and the enhancement of individual status and economic well-being. While environmental education advocates learning that is holistic and co-operative, school learning tends to be atomistic and individual. In environmental education rhetoric students are active thinkers and generators of knowledge, but in schools students are usually in the passive position of spectators and recipients of other people's knowledge and thinking. Instead of learning and action proceeding hand in hand, the acquisition of knowledge precedes its application (Fensham 1979). Finally, the mastery of relevant knowledge and skills is demonstrated in environmental education by students' actions in real situations (that is, their performance in exerting influence on environmental decision making), not by students writing about theory in artificial situations (that is, their performance in 'influencing' the teacher).

An understanding of the predominance of the practices outlined, apparently throughout most of the world, and the contradictions they create with the goals of environmental education can be gained by examining, first, the structural organisation of schools and, second, the professional ideologies that underlie teachers' organisation and transmission of knowledge.

School organisation and the need for order

As already described, historically schools have been designed for the mass processing and credentialling (and, some would add, the child minding) of children and adolescents. They require one adult to interact all day in a confined space with one (in primary schools) or several different (in secondary schools) large group(s) of students whose attendance is coerced. Teachers' work with these groups is defined, to a large extent, by the demands of an assessment system which measures students' mastery of a broad range of standardised content (so that the academic performance of students across the state or country can be compared). Therefore, to be regarded as an effective teacher (by the majority of school authorities, colleagues, parents and students, as well as even oneself), the efficient coverage of material is necessary. Together, the organisational conditions and the demand for covering material compel teachers to be concerned, first and foremost, with maintaining order and control in their classrooms.

This concern is most obviously manifested in the many classrooms where teachers agree to make minimal demands of their students in exchange for their compliant behaviour (McNeil 1983; Powell, Farrar & Cohen 1985; Sedlak et al. 1986). Yet even the dominance of teacher talk can be attributed not only to the desire to dispense information, but also to the control of classroom interaction which it facilitates (Schrag, in press). Further evidence of the frequent subordination of educational goals to social control comes from observations of teachers who immediately decrease the degree of difficulty and increase the amount of structure of classroom tasks when confronted with management problems (Doyle 1983).

Consequently, for many teachers a major criterion in deciding on pedagogical strategies and in selecting student tasks is that they are unlikely to create control problems. And highly structured tasks which are unambiguous and have single correct answers or solutions (such as the mechanistic application of algorithms or other given information) tend to meet this criterion. Such tasks fulfil two other essential criteria for teachers: ease of marking and grading (which is an important consideration, especially for secondary teachers who often have well over a hundred students) and, more significantly, ease of justifying the grading to both students and parents (Schrag, in press). Given the school's role in credentialling students and determining their future opportunities by means of competitive grading and ranking, pressures are placed on teachers and school administrators to use an assessment system which is perceived to be fair and objective. Only a system which is readily understood and accepted by the majority of students and parents is likely to be so perceived. Teachers face much greater difficulty in convincing students of the fairness of grading criteria when they assign 'ill-structured' problems, which are characterised by ambiguous definition and indeterminate criteria for solution (Simon 1973). As a result, assessment systems emphasise the mastery of selected fragments of knowledge and skills developed by well-structured tasks. And technically, of course, it is easier to test for such knowledge and skills.

Additional advantages of the type of learning tasks that dominate students' work in schools are their sole reliance on the teacher as a knowlege source and the short blocks of time in which they can be completed. The former negates any need for students to have access to environments and resources beyond the classroom, and the latter is highly compatible with the time schedule (i.e. approximately forty-five minute blocks) on which secondary schools function. The task of solving environmental problems, however, is not amenable to these space and time restrictions. Students need the time and freedom, for example, to visit the site of environmental conflicts and to consult local citizens, experts and libraries.

Compared with the typical school tasks, engaging students in problematic inquiry, as demanded by the goals and principles of environmental education, is a far more risky endeavour in terms of maintaining order and control. The complex problem solving and critical thinking involved in such inquiry demand of students considerable tolerance for ambiguity and uncertainty, autonomy for making judgments, and the confidence and insight to challenge conventional wisdom (Newmann 1987). In addition to being intellectually demanding, this kind of work is not appealing to many students (or adults), because it does not provide them with any immediate feeling of satisfaction or accomplishment:

> Even in the most supportive settings, humans have great difficulty subjecting their own beliefs to continuous scrutiny, difficulty in resolving ambiguity and contradiction, difficulty in sustaining interest in abstract issues of social justice, especially when criticism highlights negative features in the human condition. (Newmann 1985, p. 11)

Difficulty, ambiguity, contradiction, autonomy, and cognitive and psychological uneasiness suggest a recipe for classroom disorder rather than classroom order. If critical inquiry into and analysis of environmental situations, and the development and implementation of action strategies, were accompanied by continuous, constructive and lengthy dialogue with students, often on a one-to-one basis, then students might cope with the above characteristics. Obviously, however, the organisational conditions (class size, teacher load, time schedule, etc.) in virtually all schools are not conducive to such intensive and personalised dialogue.

Given the organisational constraints outlined, it is not surprising that teachers fail to engage students in critical and reflective analyses of environmental issues. Their need to maintain order and award grades on a competitive and objectively perceived basis evokes an avoidance of controversy and critique and instead encourages an emphasis on knowledge which represents consensus and certainty rather than conflict and ambiguity.

Teachers' curriculum and pedagogical ideologies

Besides the organisational pressures, teachers' views about knowledge and teaching (that is, their epistemological and pedagogical beliefs) are likely to influence what form of knowledge is selected and how that knowledge is then organised and transmitted in the classroom (Young 1981). In order to analyse the significance of this process it is necessary to first discuss the different forms of knowledge and ways of knowing.

Esland (1971) has described two forms of knowledge that underlie the pedagogical process. In one, knowledge is characterised as discrete, empirically tested and objective (i.e. value free). This form of knowledge is also measurable by 'explicit and public criteria' (Popkewitz, Tabachnick & Wehlage 1982). The other form is more subjective, problematic and essentially personal in nature, being socially constructed from the learner's active participation in the production and verification of meaning. These different conceptions of knowledge are analogous to two of Habermas's (1971) areas of cognitive interest or assumptions about what constitutes legitimate knowledge, namely the technical and the practical. The technical way of knowing results from objective inquiry associated with the empirical-analytic sciences and is intended to serve the human activity of work, leading in modern technological societies to the professionalisation and compartmentalisation of (scientific) knowledge in specialist disciplines. The practical way of knowing, according to Habermas, emerges from the historical-hermeneutic sciences which are concerned with generating knowledge in order to interpret communicative or social interactional experience.

Given the above distinction and language, the dominant conception of knowledge in schools can be categorised as authoritative, objective, discipline-centred and technical. The prevalence of this form of knowledge has been attributed to: (1) teachers' (often subconscious) presupposition (Robottom 1982) that it is the only—or at least the only legitimate— type (usually a result of their own educational experiences); (2) the process of teacher socialisation whereby professional competence is defined by one's mastery of a subject (for secondary teachers) or by one's pedagogical expertise within a traditional curriculum and instructional system (for primary teachers); and (3) the effect of numerous messages conveyed by society that it has the highest status (Young 1971). In any case, the school's role of 'objectively' assessing and credentialling individuals provides a powerful pressure to acknowledge only this epistemological position.

Exclusive adherence to the objective view of knowledge supports the concern for maintaining classroom order. It enables the teacher to exercise cognitive authority by owning and controlling the confirmation and disconfirmation of classroom knowledge, as evidenced by teachers' transformation of student discourse into the language of formal knowledge (Young 1980). In this way the teacher can control course content and the communication process in the classroom, especially when the recitation method is supported with highly structured materials (usually texts) which enable the 'teacher to specify the activity that each pupil should be engaging in at any one time' (Young 1980, p. 63). The more personal, subjective and practical knowledge form creates a place for commonsense knowledge acquired from everyday experience and therefore, by recognising their epistemological system (Everhart 1983), transfers some cognitive control to students. This transfer makes the direction of student participation more unpredictable and thereby renders the teacher's social control more problematic.

Bernstein (1975) has argued that teachers' pedagogical approaches are related to their approaches to curriculum organisation and student assessment, as well as to their desired degree of control of classroom processes. His theory predicts that in a subject-centred curriculum, pedagogy will focus on the acquisition of concepts and ideas associated with distinct disciplines and assessment will use explicit subject-derived criteria to measure students' degree of mastery of pre-specified knowledge and skills. A problem-centred or interdisciplinary curriculum, as entailed in environmental education, creates problems for teachers in curriculum organisation, pedagogical control (i.e. in demarcating the place of students' personal knowledge as described above), and the assessment of student learning (i.e. alternative criteria and modes of evaluation have to be derived) (Bernstein 1975).

Strong support for Bernstein's theory is provided by a study of 152 teachers in five Australian secondary schools, which found a significant correlation between teachers' beliefs in a subject-centred curriculum, a competitive and 'objective' assessment process, and a high degree of control over classroom interactions (Young 1981). The study also revealed that this profile of teacher ideology was associated with an objectivist view of knowledge. Consequently, the author concluded that 'teachers' epistemologies are an important part of their pedagogical ideologies and are therefore likely to be involved in the shaping of teachers' pedagogical practices' (Young 1981, p. 204).

The nature of current school curriculum, therefore, can be related to teachers' professional ideologies and the 'institutionalisation of dominant beliefs about knowledge, teaching and learning' (McIntyre 1985, p. 79). The significance of the latter effect was recognised at the Tbilisi international conference when a research need in environmental education was identified as 'determining the obstacles the (epistemological, cultural or social) restricting access to educational messages and their utilization' (Tbilisi Declaration 1978, p. 28).

Introducing environmental education into a school challenges the dominant conception, organisation and transmission of knowledge, creating for most teachers a conflict with their approach to teaching and learning (Esland 1971). Treating knowledge and its transmission as problematic creates a new definition of the role of the teacher and demands changes in the organisational conditions under which teachers generally work. If environmental education in its contemporary form is ever to become a reality in schools, then these two issues must seriously be addressed.

Notes

1 I am grateful to Fred Newmann, Joe Onosko, Tom Popkewitz and Fran Schrag for their thoughtful comments on an earlier draft of this paper.

2 This typology represents an adaption of the work of Enzensberger (1974), in particular, and Huckle (1983).

References

Apple, M. W. (1979), *Ideology and Curriculum*, Routledge & Kegan Paul, London.

Apple, M. W. (1982), *Education and Power*, Routledge & Kegan Paul, Boston, Mass.

Attfield, R. (1983), *The Ethics of Environmental Concern*, Columbia University Press, New York.

Barnes, D. (1969), *From Communication to Curriculum*, Penguin, Harmondsworth.

Barnes, D. (1976), *Language, the Learner and the School*, Penguin, Harmondsworth.

Belgrade Charter (1976) in P. Fensham, *A Report on the Belgrade Workshop on Environmental Education*, Curriculum Development Centre, Canberra.

Bellack, A., Kliebard, H. M., Hyman, R. T., & Smith, F. L. (1966), *The Language of the Classroom*, Teachers College Press, New York.

Bernstein, B. (1975), *Class, Codes and Control*, vol. 3, Routledge & Kegan Paul, London.

Carson, R. (1962), *Silent Spring*, Houghton Mifflin, Boston, Mass.

Childress, R. B. (1978), 'Public school environmental education curricula: A national profile', *The Journal of Environmental Education* 9(3), 2–11.

Cusick, P. A. (1977), *Inside High School: The Student's World*, Holt, Rinehart & Winston, New York.

Devall, W., & Sessions, G. (1985), *Deep Ecology: Living as if Nature Mattered*, Peregrine Smith, Salt Lake City, UT.

Doyle, W. (1983), 'Academic work', *Review of Educational Research* 53(2), 159–99.

Durkheim, E. (1956), *Education and Sociology*, Free Press, New York.

Enzensberger, H. M. (1974), 'A critique of political ecology', *New Left Review* (84), 3–31.

Esland, G. (1971), 'Teaching and learning as the organization of knowledge', in M. F. D. Young, *Knowledge and Control: New Directions for the Sociology of Education*, Collier-Macmillan, London.

Everhart, R. B. (1983), *Reading, Writing and Resistance: Adolescence and Labor in a Junior High School*, Routledge & Kegan Paul, Boston, Mass.

Fensham, P. (1979), 'Educating a community for its environmental situations', in *1980 Plus: Community, Participation and Learning*, (Book 4), Australian Association for Community Education and Planning Services Division of the Education Department of Victoria, Melbourne.

Fox, W. (1984), 'Towards a deeper ecology?', *Habitat Australia* 13(4), 26–8.

Goodlad, J. I. (1984), *A Place Called School*, McGraw-Hill, New York.

Greenall, A. (1981), 'Environmental education: A case study in national curriculum action', *Environmental Education and Information* 1(4), 285–94.

Habermas, J. (1971), *Knowledge and Human Interests*, Beacon Press, Boston, Mass.

Huckle, J. (1983), 'Environmental education', in J. Huckle (ed.), *Geographical Education: Reflection and Action*, Oxford University Press, Oxford.

Kliebard, H. M. (1977), 'The Tyler rationale', in A. A. Bellack & H. M. Kliebard (eds), *Curriculum and Evaluation*, McCutchan, Berkeley, Calif.

Leopold, A. (1948), *A Sand County Almanac*, Tamarack Press, Madison, Wis.

Lundgren, U. P. (1981), *Education as a Context for Work*, Reports on Education and Psychology no.1, Department of Educational Research, Institute of Education, Stockholm.

Maher, M. (1982), Obstacles to environmental education: A hegemonic hypothesis, Paper presented at the Second National Conference of the Australian Association for Environmental Education, Brisbane.

Maher, M. (1986), 'Environmental education: What are we fighting for?', *Geographical Education* 5(2), 21–5.

McIntyre, J. (1985), *Schooling and the Management of Knowledge* (EED422 Sociology of Education), Deakin University, Vic.

McNeil, L. M. (1983), 'Defensive teaching and classroom control', in M.W. Apple & J.L. Weis (eds), *Ideology and Practice in Schools*, Temple University Press, Philadelphia, Pa.

Newmann, F. M. (1975), *Education for Citizen Action*, McCutchan, Berkeley, Calif.

Newmann, F. M. (1985), 'The radical perspective on social studies: A synthesis and critique', *Theory and Research in Social Education* 13(1), 1–18.

Newmann, F. M. (1987), Higher order thinking in the high school curriculum, Paper presented at the Annual Meeting of the National Association of Secondary School Principals, San Antonio, Tex.

Newmann, F. M., Bertocci, T. A., & Landsness, R. M. (1977), *Skills in Citizen Action: An English-Social Studies Program for Secondary Schools*, National Textbook Company, Skokie, Ill.

O'Riordan, T. (1981), 'Environmental issues', *Progress in Human Geography* **5**(3), 393–407.

Popkewitz, T. S. (1983), *Change and Stability in Schooling: The Dual Quality of Educational Reform* (ESA841 *Theory and Practice in Educational Administration*), Deakin University, Vic.

Popkewitz, T. S., Tabachnick, B. R., & Wehlage, G. (1982), *The Myth of Educational Reform: A Study of School Responses to a Program of Change*, University of Wisconsin Press, Madison, Wis.

Powell, A. G., Farrar, E., & Cohen, D. K. (1985), *The Shopping Mall High School*, Houghton Mifflin, Boston, Mass.

Reid, A. (1980), 'The essence of environmental education', *Australian Association for Environmental Education Newsletter* (1), April 1980, 3–6.

Robottom, I. M. (1982), What is: Environmental education as education about the environment, Paper presented at the Second National Conference of the Australian Association for Environmental Education, Brisbane.

Robottom, I. M. (1983), *The Environmental Education Project Evaluation Report*, Curriculum Development Centre, Canberra/ Deakin University, Vic.

Robottom, I. M. (1985), Contestation and continuity in educational reform: A critical study of innovations in environmental education, Unpublished PhD thesis, School of Education, Deakin University, Vic.

Schrag, F. (in press), *Thinking in School and Society*, Routledge & Kegan Paul, New York.

Sedlak, M. W., Wheeler, C. W., Pullin, D. C., & Cusick, P. A. (1986), *Selling Students Short*, Teachers College Press, New York.

Sizer, T. R. (1984), *Horace's Compromise: The Dilemma of the American High School*, Houghton Mifflin, Boston, Mass.

Simon, H. A. (1973), 'The structure of ill-structured problems', *Artificial Intelligence* 3–4 (Winter), 181–201.

Stapp, W. B. (1974), 'Historical setting of environmental education', in J. A. Swan & W. B. Stapp (eds), *Environmental Education: Strategies Toward a More Livable Future*, Sage, New York.

Stevenson, R. B. (1984), Curriculum materials for U.S. and Australian schools: An explanation of the theory–practice gap in environmental education?, Paper presented at the Thirteenth Annual Conference of the North American Association for Environmental Education, Chateau Lake Louise, Alberta.

Strom, A. A. (1980), 'The development of environmental education', *Australian Association for Environmental Education Newsletter* (2), July 1980, 4–5.

Tanner, R. T. (1974), *Ecology, Environment and Education*, Professional Educators Publications, Lincoln, Nebr.

Tbilisi Declaration (1978), in *Toward an Action Plan: A Report on the Tbilisi Intergovernmental Conference on Environmental Education*, US Government Printing Office, Washington, DC.

United Nations Educational, Scientific and Cultural Organization (1977), *Education and the Challenge of Environmental Problems*, UNESCO, Paris.

Volk, T. L., Hungerford, H. R., & Tomera, A. N. (1984), 'A national survey of curriculum needs as perceived by professional environmental educators', *The Journal of Environmental Education* **16**(1), 10–19.

Wheeler, K. (1975), 'The genesis of environmental education', in G. C. Martin & K. Wheeler (eds), *Insights into Environmental Education*, Oliver Boyd, Edinburgh.

Young, M. F. D. (1971), *Knowledge and Control: New Directions for the Sociology of Education*, Collier-Macmillan, London.

Young, R. E. (1980), 'The controlling curriculum and the practical ideology of teachers', *The Australian and New Zealand Journal of Sociology* **16**(2), 62–70.

Young, R. E. (1981), 'A study of teacher epistemologies', *The Australian Journal of Education* **25**(2), 194–208.

Annotated bibliography

Enzensberger, H. M. 'A critique of political ecology'. *New Left Review*, no. 84, 1974, pp. 3–31.

Enzensberger delineates three groups involved in the environmental movement of the early 1970s, each of which is appraised in terms of its underlying ideology. He questions the claimed social neutrality of all three and argues that their rhetoric conceals and promotes various economic and political interests. For example, the demands of developed countries for population control in the Third World are described as containing the idealogical motive of a fear that population pressure will become a source of political and military power. Ecologists' discussion of the 'spaceship earth' or global ecosystem concept is revealed as denying class contradictions and domination by failing to address the global distribution of resources. The author convincingly illustrates how ecological doomsdayers (such as the Ehrlichs) depoliticise the crisis they describe through their unwillingness to question the need for radical changes in our social and economic system. Yet ecological equilibrium cannot be restored without giving attention to the decisive social components and consequences.

Everhart, R. B. *Reading, Writing and Resistance: Adolescence and Labor in a Junior High School*. Routledge & Kegan Paul, Boston, Mass., 1983.

This ethnographic study reveals the contradictions between the knowledge system sanctioned by a school and that associated with the cultural world of adolescents. Using Habermas's framework, Everhart contrasts the school's 'recipe' knowledge, over which students had 'little control as to its form and consequence', with the socially constructed (and reconstructed) knowledge created in students' non-academic group activities, where meanings and values emerged from their interactions. He suggests that students' epistemology serves as a type of resistance to, or more accurately escape from, school-based knowledge. This analysis provokes the question: How might schools constructively incorporate into their curriculum and teaching the process of constructing meaning that is involved in the students' knowledge system?

Newmann, F. M. *Education for Citizen Action*. McCutchan, Berkeley, Calif., 1975.

This book provides a comprehensive rationale for the need to increase individual competence to exert influence on public decision making on social and (by extension) environmental issues. Newmann argues that action or participation alone is not the educational aim; the ability to produce outcomes consistent with the individual's intentions is equally important. The rationale is based on three major lines of argument: (1) satisfaction of a fundamental psychological need to exercise competence through exerting influence on one's environment, (2) the principle of 'consent of the governed', which requires that each citizen have equal opportunity to affect the use of political power, and (3) the need to possess the competence to act on a situation in order to experience an authentic moral dilemma.

This sound educational rationale should help alleviate the concerns of many teachers and administrators about justifying the involvement of students in taking environmental action. Furthermore, it provides a justification that is not dependent on the political activism embodied in the international environmental education rhetoric.

Towards inquiry-based professional development in environmental education

Ian Robottom

Introduction

THIS ESSAY PRESENTS an argument for a two-fold reform in the teaching of environmental education in formal education settings.[1] Firstly, it argues that just as environmental education programs (and the students in those programs) ought to adopt an environmentally and socially critical orientation in the investigation of environmental problems with a view to the improvement of the environment, so provision ought to be made to allow teachers of environmental education to adopt a similarly critical form of educational inquiry in the investigation of the problems of environmental education program improvement.

Secondly, it argues that conventional approaches to program and professional development in environmental education misrepresent the educational problem posed by substantial innovations in education, and suggests that environmental improvement and environmental education improvement are both *political* matters that tend to be depoliticised by the adoption of an applied science perspective.

The essay begins with some key statements from the literature of the International Environmental Education Programme launched by the United Nations Educational, Scientific and Cultural Organization (UNESCO) in 1975 in co-operation with the United Nations Environmental Programme (UNEP).[2] These statements reflect some of the more political concerns of the times and lay the basis for a statement of the challenge confronting environmental education in the 1980s. After a survey of the international orgins of contemporary environmental education, three examples of environmental education organisation within the infrastructure of the environmental education movement are examined, and it is suggested that rationalist, technocratic approaches to professional development are inappropriate responses to the challenge confronting environmental education in formal education settings. A reconstruction of the educational problem of reform in environmental education then follows, and an alternative approach to professional development in environmental education is proposed. Finally, the essay's position on this issue is summarised, and some guiding principles for professional development in environmental education are suggested.

Some messages from the UNESCO program

The 1980s mark a checkpoint in environmental education activities. As we enter the second decade after the landmark events of the UNESCO program of the 1970s, it is time to look retrospectively at environmental education in the light of those events and prospectively at environmental education as we prepare for the 1990s and beyond.

The comments of Adriano Buzzati-Traverso, who was Senior Scientific Advisor to UNEP and a key figure in the UNESCO program in the mid-1970s, are even more relevant in this information age of the mid-1980s. In a UNESCO document, he states:

> At any one time, the educational system—whether based on religious dogmas and practices or on rational thought—has tried to divulge, sustain and perpetuate sets of social values. The process has occurred sometimes openly, at other times through devious channels. If you consider the world today and examine the diverse educational systems, you can clearly identify competing ideologies: those which are attempting to hold on to recognized and almost undisputed values, and those which have launched a major strategy for conquering the world and men's [and women's] minds.
>   In other terms, behind any educational process lies a philosophy, a moral philosophy, for the people who exert power and are in charge of educational institutions share certain values, which they wish to disseminate in order to ensure the prolongation, if not the indefinite survival, of the system they are devoted to. (Buzzati-Traverso 1977, p. 14)

In environmental education, when we are focusing on environmental issues, we are aware that various self-interests 'contest the ground' (we are prepared to become quite angry when we believe that some industries and governments are exploiting the environment). Buzzati-Traverso's comments remind us that education is ideological— that individual, group and corporate self-interests are at work in any educational endeavour. In other words, the very *educational processes* by which environmental issues are studied are also subject to the influence and struggles of a range of self-interests.

A philosophy similar to Buzzati-Traverso's is discernible in some of the rhetoric which emerged from the next landmark event in the UNESCO program, the Intergovernmental Conference on Environmental Education at Tbilisi, USSR, in 1977:

> The problems of the environment are indeed complex ones. They involve numerous parameters and interrelations. Lacking the necessary knowledge and approaches, individuals admit defeat and hand the problems over to the specialists. It is in terms such as these that recourse to technocracy is frequently justified. The result is the abandonment of any attempt to involve ordinary people, who come to be regarded as mere operatives or consumers. (UNESCO 1980, p. 26)

This statement is significant because it warns us that 'recourse to technocracy' in environmental education can result in a division of labour that disenfranchises 'ordinary people' and promotes passive consumerism of information about the environment. The problem with passive consumerism is that it leaves unscrutinised the sorts of self-interests that Buzzati-Traverso warns us about. 'Recourse to technocracy' can be seen in many attempts to resolve environmental predicaments; it is equally visible in the processes of development and implementation of certain environmental education projects for schools.

The Tbilisi conference also provided some pointers to the type of mindset and activities that might overcome this passive consumerism:

> Environmental education should not confine itself to disseminating new knowledge but should help the public question its misconceptions concerning the various problems of the environment and the value systems of which these ideas are a part . . .
>   All decisions regarding the development of society and the improvement of the lot of individuals are based on considerations, usually implicit, concerning what is useful, good, beautiful and so on. The educated individual should be in a position to ask such questions as: Who took this decision? According to what criteria? With what immediate ends in mind? Have the long-term consequences been calculated? In short, he [or she] must know what choices have been made and what value system determined them. (UNESCO 1980, pp. 26–7)

Environmental education should go beyond the exploration of the realities that are constructed by particular individuals and groups at particular times to look also at questions about *how* and *why* reality comes to be constructed in these particular ways.

The three quoted passages, extracted from the international environmental education literature of the past decade, contain three main messages:

1 While we recognise that environmental issues serve certain self-interests, we should also recognise that all *educational processes* serve certain *self-interests*.

2 There is a tendency in environmental education to adopt a *technocratic* approach to the resolution of environmental issues and educational problems, and such an approach promotes *passive consumerism* in both environmental problem solving and educational problem solving.

3 Environmental education should not restrict itself to technocratic solutions but should adopt an approach that is *critical* and *participatory*, seeking out the self-interests that shape the environmental predicaments and educational processes that figure in our environmental education work.

Environmental education is not easy work. Clearly there are difficulties in reaching a stage where environmental education is institutionalised in formal education.

At the school level, environmental education poses significant curriculum and teaching problems for practitioners: it aspires to be interdisciplinary, but the conventional school curriculum is strongly disciplinary; it entails outdoor education, but school rules and regulations impose constraints on out-of-classroom activities; it is a form of inquiry teaching, but structures and relationships in schools tend to reproduce more didactic forms of instruction; it is interested in inquiries that are critical, involving critiques of environmental situations, but schooling tends to be more interested in vocational or liberal education.

The next section of this essay traces the international origins of contemporary environmental education and suggests that the key influences in institutional education that have shaped the development of environmental education embody a number of tensions and contradictions.

The technocratisation of environmental education

International origins of contemporary environmental education

> By the laws of nature man cannot live without food. Whatever may be the rate at which population would increase if unchecked, it never can actually increase in any country beyond the food necessary to support it. (Malthus 1972, p. 83)

Thomas Malthus (1766–1834), a pioneer in the treatment of demographic problems, raised early environmental concerns. His thesis – that population, when unchecked, increases in geometrical ratio while subsistence increases in arithmetical ratio – prompted concerns about the relationship of population growth rates and 'quality of life'. While many other early examples of increasing awareness of environmental problems may be found (see, for example, Liebmann 1973), they are not the concern of this essay; here we are concerned with those events of the 1960s and onwards which created the sharpest images of environmental crisis.

Rachel Carson's disturbing book, *Silent Spring* (1962), prompted widespread debate and activities in the community about the preservation of the environment in the light of perceived *pollution* problems, especially those concerning pesticides. Her message was that the mass production of pesticide pollutants, such as DDT and lead compounds, and their widespread use around the world, is endangering the biosphere. On 24 December 1968, the spacecraft Apollo 8 beamed to the world clear photographs depicting the Earth in limitless black space. For the first time, men and women throughout the world were shown dramatic symbolic evidence of the finite nature of Earth's resources:

> For the first time men and women realized the limitations of the earth's resources, the delicate balance of forces which have made Earth inhabitable, and the inevitable consequences of man's continuing prodigality. For the first time, they understood what the environmentalists, conservationists, and ecologists had been trying to convey. (Tuttle 1976, p.v)

Some of these 'environmentalists, conservationists, and ecologists' who helped raise community consciousness about the relationship between population, resources and environment before and after Apollo 8 were Holdren and Ehrlich (1971), Commoner (1971), and Meadows et al. (1972). Holdren and Ehrlich present an eloquent perspective of the world of their day:

> The world faces today a multiplicity of crises: explosive political and ideological conflicts, rampant malnutrition, grinding poverty, and inexorable erosion of the capacity of the natural environment to support life. These extant and potential disasters are inextricably entwined with each other and with a global population size and growth rate unprecedented in the tenure of *Homo sapiens* on Earth. Together they preclude a humane and fruitful existence for a considerable fraction of the world's inhabitants, they bid fair to destroy such worthwhile values as today's civilization may embody, and in their most sinister aspects they imperil even the habitability of the planet. (Holdren & Ehrlich 1971, p. 1)

The Club of Rome, an international group of industrialists and others, used computer projections to confirm the Malthusian proposition that population growth is exponential, and to predict that the planet is approaching the limits to which it can support this growth. The increasing public concern about environmental issues in the 1960s and 1970s can be gauged from the attempts in a number of countries to protect and enhance Earth's resources and from the formation of international community action groups such as Zero Population Growth and Friends of the Earth. In 1968, the British Society for Social Responsibility in Science was established, its main aim being 'to stimulate among scientists an awareness of the social significance of science, and of the scientist's corresponding responsibility towards society' (Fuller 1971, inside front cover). At its international conference in 1970, the society not only acknowledged serious environmental problems, but also discussed at length the relationship between those problems, society and the structure of scientific research traditions (see, for example, Hancock 1971).

The late 1960s and early 1970s also saw increasing international grass-roots concern about the ability of science to handle those environmental problems (see Smolicz 1974). For Malcolm, this was the

> . . . era of the antiscience movement, the environmentalist movement, the antiwar movement and movements to liberate blacks, women and homosexuals. It was reaction against exploitation for economic 'progress', against mass distribution and mass control, including mass schooling. It was a cultural exhortation for recognition of individuality and individual worth. (Malcolm 1984, p. 8)

In response to this environmental consciousness at the international grass-roots level, the United Nations became increasingly concerned with questions about population, resources and the environment, and in 1972 organised the United Nations Conference on the Human Environment which was held in Stockholm.

The Stockholm conference was a landmark in that it signalled a degree of international unity in the recognition of, and concern about, population, resources and the environment. There was sufficient evidence to establish that environmental problems transcend national frontiers (Fensham 1978) and that the environmental crisis is global. The conference heard statements concerning issues which were not only environmental and international, but also sharply *political*. For example:

> The need to conserve rapidly dwindling resources must be associated with concern for the majority of the world's population which has not yet had its share.
>
> A minority of countries and of the world's population account for the majority of its energy consumption and produce most of its pollution. However, these are concomitants of a standard of living not yet enjoyed by the majority, who might rightly aspire to much of it.
>
> There are very real threats to the continual existence of unique aspects of the natural order and humanity's historic heritage. The immediate environment of millions would be regarded by many others as quite intolerable. (Fensham 1978, pp. 446-7)

It is worth reiterating that the United Nations' involvement in environmental education was a *response to*, rather than an *initiator of*, the worldwide, grass-roots concern about the environment (Fensham 1984). And, while environment-related activities *were* offered in schools at that time in the form of nature studies and outdoor education programs, these tended to be an outcome of the liberal-progressive educational philosophies of Dewey and others[3] and were politically, if not historically, independent of the types of issues discussed at the Stockholm conference.

The Stockholm conference also marked the beginning of a concerted, long-term involvement by the United Nations in the development of an international program in environmental education. The resultant UNESCO program, headed by Professor William Stapp, of the University of Michigan, convened an international workshop on environmental education in Belgrade in October, 1975. About a hundred educational specialists from 64 countries took part in the workshop, which aimed to review the trends and emerging issues in environmental education and to formulate guidelines and recommendations for advancing the movement internationally (Stapp 1978). Discussions at the workshop were to be based on the results of an internationally administered, questionnaire-based needs survey, and on commissioned 'trend-papers'.[4]

But the workshop agenda was disturbed in what turned out to be a positive way. After an initial working party on 'the concept and philosophy of environmental education', a plenary session was scheduled to 'pull the threads together'. Instead, a Latin American delegate succeeded in launching a debate about 'the environmental situation' – the context in which the workshop was planning environmental education. The debate exposed a number of political elements, including the notions of 'developed/developing countries' and 'aid' between countries. It raised the profile of some of the issues discussed at Stockholm and resulted in what Australian delegate Peter Fensham later described as 'an incredibly creative situation' (Fensham 1984). Thanks to the persistence of the Latin Americans and the flexibility of the organisers, a two-day hiatus in the formal proceedings of the workshop allowed the more or less spontaneous expression of a groundswell of international community opinion, the culmination of which was an unexpected and strongly-supported document, the Belgrade Charter. The initial statement of the charter, entitled 'Environmental Situation', captures the political edge which most delegates apparently saw as essential to the notion of environmental education they were to underwrite.[5] For example, there is a statement apparently directed at the issue of 'developed/developing countries' (one which could be construed, because of its concern over the distribution of resources, as having political implications):

> It is absolutely vital that the world's citizens insist upon measures that will support the kind of economic growth which will not have harmful repercussions on people – that will not in any way diminish their environment and their living conditions. It is necessary to find ways to ensure that no nation should grow or develop at the expense of another nation and that the consumption of no individual should be increased at the expense of other individuals. (Fensham 1976, pp. 23–4)

An even sharper perspective of the political issue of defence spending is also included in the charter:

> Above all, it [a prescribed 'new global ethic'] will demand the assurance of perpetual peace through the coexistence and co-operation between nations with different social systems. Substantial resources for reallocation to meet human needs can be gained through restricting military budgets and reducing competition in the manufacture of arms. Disarmament should be the ultimate goal. (Fensham 1976, p. 24)

When the original workshop agenda was resumed, the spirit of critique and negotiation remained. Working groups were charged with commenting on draft trend papers and making recommendations to plenary sessions for ratification as recommendations of the workshop (Fensham 1976). These trend papers, which had been prepared by 'environmental education experts' selected by UNESCO, purported to describe the worldwide state of the art in environmental education, but in the working group discussions the assumptions underpinning many of the trend papers were strongly questioned.

The Belgrade Charter, probably the most widely read outcome of the Belgrade workshop, contains elements which are at first glance descriptive but which on closer inspection show the influence of a number of divergent interests (see for example, the section in the charter on the 'Environmental Situation'). On the other hand, much of the charter is openly *prescriptive* – it is essentially an internationally formulated policy statement for the environmental education movement. The key prescriptions are (Fensham 1976, p. 26):

1 Environmental education should consider the environment in its totality – natural and man-made, ecological, political, economic, technological, social, legislative, cultural and aesthetic.
2 Environmental education should be a continuous life-long process, both in-school and out-of-school,
3 Environmental education should be interdisciplinary in its approach.
4 Environmental education should emphasise active participation in preventing and solving environmental problems.
5 Environmental education should examine major environmental issues from a world point of view, while paying due regard to regional differences.
6 Environmental education should focus on current and future environmental situations.
7 Environmental education should examine all development and growth from an environmental perspective.

8 Environmental education should promote the value and necessity of local, national and international co-operation in the solution of environmental problems.

The flexible agenda and informal working groups of the Belgrade workshop fostered a climate of creativity and volatility and provided a forum for competing views of the environmental situation and appropriate educational responses. The discourse at Belgrade was marked by contestation and negotiation, some of which was captured in the Belgrade Charter itself. To the extent that the charter has acted as an influential policy statement in the environmental education movement, the workshop responsible for its development earns 'landmark' status in our discussion.

Following the Belgrade workshop, the UNESCO program moved into a phase of consolidation. An international information exchange network was established by means of the newsletter *Connect* and regional meetings were convened in all five continents to examine the Belgrade Charter recommendations and to adapt them to regional needs. Like the Belgrade workshop, the regional meetings brought together experts in environmental education to advise UNESCO on the continued implementation of its program. According to UNESCO, none of the regional meetings expressed major disagreements with the spirit of the Belgrade Charter's goals and objectives for environmental education. For example, the 'objectives' statements and the list of 'guiding principles of environmental education programs' were considered valid by all regional meetings (UNESCO 1977).

The regional meetings were also seen as a form of preparation for the next major conference on environmental education which was held at Tbilisi, USSR, in October 1977. Only official delegations from United Nations member states and from organisations recognised by the United Nations attended the UNESCO-UNEP Intergovernmental Conference on Environmental Education at Tbilisi. Seventy countries were represented at the conference, the stated purpose of which was to recommend actions that could be taken at the national, regional and international levels to promote and develop environmental education (Eulefield 1979). The Tbilisi conference was a landmark in the environmental education movement because it constituted a more formal, intergovernmental recognition of the environmental education concept developed at Belgrade. As the former head of the UNESCO program secretariat, William Stapp, noted: 'The adopted policy recommendations of the conference are for all practical purposes binding on the member states (countries) and organizations present' (Stapp 1978, p. 40). The main agenda items considered by the Tbilisi conference were (Jeske 1978, p. 5):

- major environmental problems in contemporary society;
- role of education in facing the challenges of environmental problems;
- current efforts at the national and international levels for the development of environmental education;
- strategies for the development of environmental education at the national level:
  (a) general environmental education of the public through formal and nonformal education;
  (b) environmental education (including in-service education) of particular professional groups whose actions and decisions have implications for the environment;
- regional and international cooperation for the development of environmental education: needs and modalities.

As this list shows, the 'role of education' figured prominently in the thinking of conference organisers. To encourage discussion of the role of environmental education, the organisers developed a working document entitled 'Current efforts at the national and international levels for the development of environmental education'[6], which was based substantially on surveys of the five regions in which the UNESCO meetings were held between the Belgrade and the Tbilisi conferences. This document is useful in the present discussion because it provides an international perspective of the efforts made to develop environmental education during this period. Comments about *efforts in formal education* include (UNESCO 1977):

- . . . efforts [at environmental education development] differ considerably in their intensity and nature from one country to another, being focused on all or some of the following aspects . . . *inclusion* of environmental topics in education, *training* of the personnel required for the development of environmental education, *teaching materials, research* and establishment of a *national institutional framework* for environmental education. (p. 17)
- As regards *the content of curricula comprising environment-related topics*, the following general trends are to be noted: in most regions, where formal education is concerned, priority is given, at *pre-primary and primary levels*, to the natural environment, although several programmes exist in each of the regions bearing upon the social environment. (p. 17)
- At *secondary* level, the content of environmental education seems to conform very much to the same pattern and there is a tendency for it to be incorporated into traditional disciplines, such as biology and geography. (p. 18)
- . . . environment-related topics are generally dealt with in the framework of specialized disciplines; no attempt is made to give them an interdisciplinary character or to foster problem-solving or contact with the community outside the school. (p. 19)
- . . . environment-related topics are generally of an interdisciplinary nature, as specialists have more opportunity to come together around a common centre of interest. Non-formal environmental programmes relate to the actual problems of the local community and their object is to find solutions to them. (p. 19)
- Relatively few efforts have been made in any of the regions to supplement the traditional *training* of teachers, organizers of educational activities and educational administrators with a view to producing competent staff for environmental education . . . (p. 19)
- In the five regions, environment-related topics are generally included in the training of biology and geography teachers for formal education. In such cases, the main emphasis is on the principles of the conservation and protection of nature, generally at the stage of pre-service rather than in-service training. (p. 19)
- In every region, the existence of large quantities of teaching materials for environmental education has been observed. The most common are those produced for the traditional formal sector of education: books and textbooks written for courses specifically centred on the conservation of nature and which, not taking account of the interactions between the social and natural factors of the environment, continue to deal with it in a compartmentalized manner. (p. 20)
- The role of applied *research* in environmental education should be to remedy the shortcomings and gaps in [environmental] education. Although only very few activities have so far been undertaken in this field, in all regions there are signs of a will to carry out research on certain particular points. (p. 21)
- Some countries tend above all to carry out research on *teaching materials* in support of environmental education programmes in the formal and non-formal sectors. (p. 21)

These comments reveal that a number of the key influences shaping the development of environmental education have their origins in institutional education. According to UNESCO (1977), problems relating to the *interdisciplinary* nature of environmental education stem from the fact that environmental education is 'often dispensed within the framework of separate disciplines and thus presents a distorted and incomplete picture of the complicated nature of mutual interactions and influences which determine environmental issues' (p. 22). The notion of the school as a self-contained entity, isolated from society, exacerbates the difficulties of developing a community orientation in environmental education. New teaching approaches are considered necessary for 'the adoption of a *problem-oriented* approach proper to environmental education' (p. 22). The UNESCO document also cites *institutional* problems: 'The lack of adequate co-ordination, both horizontal, between the various institutions, and by topic, between the various disciplines, makes the interdisciplinary approach to environmental problems, the only approach which would be effective, very difficult'. *Pedagogical* problems cited by UNESCO include the unsuitability of *teaching materials* to the local environment, and the effect of 'rigid timetables' which 'rule out the possibility of any interaction between teachers in the different disciplines and allow pupils little time to take part in exercises aimed at solving specific problems affecting the life of the community'. The 'traditional method of assessment of scholastic performance' is considered inappropriate to the task of assessing personal development in environmental education (UNESCO 1977 p. 23).

Thus it was recognised by the participants in the UNESCO program of the 1970s that several of the program's prescriptions entailed practices which created tensions and contradictions when attempted within the entrenched structures and relationships of institutional education.

Tension and contradiction in institutionalised environmental education

Notwithstanding this early recognition of potential problems for environmental education as an innovation, organisational efforts were made at a number of levels to achieve the desired innovation without addressing the need for more fundamental reform of the context – the structures and relationships of institutional education – within which the innovation was to be located. In particular, these organisational efforts were informed by models of educational change that served to actually reinforce and reproduce, rather than challenge and reconstruct, the key features of institutional education.

At the international level

Although the international environmental education community recognised in 1977 that conventional structures and practices of institutional education could be strong shaping influences on formal environmental education, the general form of organisation ultimately recommended at Tbilisi was nevertheless managerial-hierarchical in character.

For example, in the 1977 UNESCO document referred to above, there are several recommendations about 'strategies for the development of environmental education' which assume a rationalist, objectives-based view of educational change:

> Strategies for the incorporation of environmental education in formal education should take into account the various components of the educational process, *that is to say the objectives, content and methods, teaching materials, training of personnel and research and evaluation activities.*
>
> So far as *objectives* are concerned, those pertaining to the understanding and solving of environmental problems need to be clearly included among those of education in general, at all levels and in all sectors.
>
> . . . a particular effort will have to be made to prepare appropriate *teaching materials*

to *train and retrain educators* and enable them to introduce environmental education into their teaching. (UNESCO 1977, p. 33)

Great importance is placed on the development of educational objectives and teaching materials, and educational research is to fulfil an instrumental role:

> ... it [is] necessary for *research and evaluation activities* relating to environmental education to be strengthened, so as to provide a scientific and experimental basis for innovations in this field. (UNESCO 1977, p. 33)
>
> Research and evaluation activities relating to environmental education . . . should provide useful guidelines for realigning approaches to the preparation of education and training programmes and for improving teaching materials. (UNESCO 1977, p. 43)

While recommending that practitioners become involved in research, the document conveys the notion of teachers as *technicians* carrying out instrumental-type research to test the effectiveness of activities and materials:

> ... another form of activity is of great importance, namely, the continuous qualitative and quantitative evaluation of environmental education activities with a view to constantly improving their efficiency and effectiveness.
> ... it ... seems particularly urgent for educators to receive not only general teacher training but also training in the devising of simple methods and instruments of research and evaluation enabling them to test, in the light of the objectives pursued, the effectiveness of the various components of the educational process (curricula, teaching materials, methods, etc.). (UNESCO 1977, p. 43)

The overall view of educational change recommended by the UNESCO program is a centre-periphery strategy, which retains the characteristics of the rationalist research, development, dissemination and adoption (RDDA) model:

> Emphasis has already been laid on the importance of research and experimentation with a view to the *preparation of curricula, methods and material which corresponds to the demands of environmental education.* In this connection, it seems necessary to undertake experimental projects which could serve as convincing examples to persuade the authorities, the teachers and the learners themselves of the possibility of developing interdisciplinary environmental education with a view to the solution and prevention of immediate problems, and which would encourage the participation of the communities concerned. But such projects usually require large-scale technical support and specialized staff who are familiar with the experiments conducted in various countries; and, as many Member States do not have the necessary resources at their disposal, it is the *role of international co-operation to stimulate the launching of such pilot projects.* It would however be necessary to see that the cost and complexity of these projects do not prevent other countries from applying any useful lessons that may be drawn from them. (UNESCO 1977, p. 52)

This statement clearly indicates the theory of social change that underpins the form of organisation advocated by UNESCO. It reiterates the emphasis on curriculum materials produced in one site and designed, with the assistance of research and experimentation, to 'be convincing', to 'persuade', and to 'encourage' other educators, learners and interested parties at other sites. Such projects, the document maintains, are cost- and labour-intensive, and require 'specialized staff' – they involve a division of labour between expert, knowledgeable developers and passive, persuadable practitioners. These are all characteristics of a rationalist RDDA model of educational change.

The form of organisation advocated by the UNESCO program is managerial-hierarchical in that it creates a hierarchy of 'managers' and 'technicians'. The managers (academia, researchers, developers) devise the language of the innovation and seek to control (by 'persuading', or 'convincing') the educational practice of the passive technicians. The language is given high priority and, once in place, provides those responsible for the organisation of the innovation with a set of directives with which to shape the practice of teachers.

But given a managerial-hierarchical form of organisation, *control over language* at one level becomes *power over decision-making, resources and practices* at other levels.

An example of an attempt to control the language of environmental education can be seen in the determined efforts of Hungerford and his associates to defend their own interpretation of the definition and aims of environmental education in a prominent international journal by admonishing the journal's editors for attempting to open up debate about the intentions and structure of environmental education (Hungerford, Peyton & Wilke 1983). In a managerial-hierarchical educational organisation, such a bid for control over language is tantamount to a bid for control over teachers' practice. Institutionalised language becomes binding policy that shapes and constrains practice. For example, at a recent international environmental education conference, Iozzi claimed 'proven effective' status for a set of environmental education strategies (Iozzi 1984). These strategies are consistent with the language of the developers and have allegedly been 'proven effective' relative to their goals by the type of instrumental educational research referred to in the UNESCO document quoted above.

But if institutional language becomes binding policy that shapes and constrains practice, teachers have very little recourse in the event of difficulties arising in the implementation of the strategies. Acceptance of the 'authoritative' language and the practices it apparently sanctions diminishes the likelihood of individuals engaging the theory of the strategies – as we have seen in the example of Hungerford and his associates, individuals who query the goals of environmental education may be publicly admonished. Nor can teachers claim that the materials are in some sense deficient or inappropriate to their setting, since the universal effectiveness of the materials is claimed to be 'proven'. The only remaining 'explanation' is that the teachers themselves are in some sense 'deficient' or 'incapable'. These organisational notions of managed change, controlled knowledge (in the form of definitions and goals), 'teacher-proof' materials, power hierarchies, and 'teacher-deficit' explanations of innovation failure conflict strongly with statements elsewhere in UNESCO documents which point to the specific, context-dependent problems associated with environmentally and socially critical environmental education. For example, under 'Some problems affecting the development of environmental education' the UNESCO document speaks of problems resulting from attempts to teach interdisciplinary environmental education in a 'framework of separate disciplines' and observes that 'the adoption of a *problem-oriented* approach proper to environmental education is made difficult by the fact that education overlooks the complexity of real life for theoretical, abstract studies' and a number of other *institutional* problems (UNESCO 1977, p. 22).

So at the international level, the adoption of a managerial-hierarchical approach to organising the innovation reinforced certain conditions – for example, a sharp division of labour between researchers and practitioners – that acted as an impediment to the educational reform necessitated by interdisciplinary, inquiry-based, socially critical environmental education. As we shall see, similar tensions and contradictions are evident at the national level as well.

At the national level

The next two recent examples of conflict in the organisation of environmental education are drawn from the national level, one in Australia and one in the United States
of America.

An Australian example

In Australia, the Curriculum Development Centre's (CDC) Environmental Education
Project (EEP) is this country's most extensive national environmental education effort
(see Robottom 1983). The project was completed in 1981 with the appearance of the
last of the five publications that form its curriculum resource kit (EEP 1980–1981).

The origins of the EEP lie in some four years of extensive deliberation and negotiation at the CDC about environmental education and an appropriate curriculum model
for dealing with it. The model adopted for the EEP sought to preserve a co-ordinating
role for the central agency, while the materials development phase aimed to encourage
interaction with practising teachers.

The EEP intended to tap instances of 'tried-and-true' environmental education
programs operating in the schools, to edit, package and publish centrally the resultant
manuscripts, and to circulate the published accounts among the schools. The process
of tapping environmental education in schools was facilitated by an incentive scheme
of small grants (up to $500) administered by the CDC from EEP funds. Individuals
involved in environmental education could apply for an advertised grant to prepare
a manuscript describing their involvement. The main criterion for the allocation of
a grant was the extent to which an applicant's description of environmental education
activities contributed to the CDC's own view of environmental education. In addition
to the manuscripts from the grants scheme, some manuscripts were commissioned.
'The resulting descriptions and analyses of activities passed through a range of trialling,
vetting and editing services which involved teachers, the [project's] Advisory Committee, the State Liaison Officer network and the management procedures convened
by the Centre' (Skilbeck 1981, p.v).

The state liaison officer network was a significant component in the project's operations. The project team included a state liaison officer to represent each state and
Territory and to act as an intermediary between the authors and the project director.
Because the CDC wanted to adopt a relatively low profile in the development and dissemination of the materials, the responsibility for dissemination, in particular, was
delegated to the states. It was intended that the state liaison officers would be able
to employ their own consultancy and resources support networks for dissemination
purposes.

As the development agency in this enterprise, the CDC had conflicting interests – it
wanted to preserve a worthwhile central role in the development of curriculum materials,
while at the same time recognising the importance of the school-based curriculum
development movement. Since it also wanted to delegate responsibility for materials
development and dissemination to the states, project operations were run by a team
comprising representatives of the state education systems. These representatives were
not closely involved in the negotiations and deliberations about the reform effort (the
innovation and appropriate curriculum responses) that took place over the previous
four years at the 'development agency' level of organisation (the CDC). That is, there
was a *disjunction in discourse* – the project team inherited the *terminology* of the reform
effort without having been party to the negotiations and discourse which shaped the

particular agreed *meaning* of the reform.

It could be argued that the process of invoking and strengthening the role of existing systems by seconding education department representatives to act as key project operatives is an example of a conflict of interests in the reform effort. The fact that responsibilities were devolved to the state level could be said to have legitimated their prior conventional *modus operandi* – the project team members were chosen *because* they were representatives of networks with contacts and expertise in materials development and dissemination. Further, it may be in the interests of systems representatives to *continue* to operate in conventional ways – even in the 'new' context of a reform effort.

The CDC was severely constrained in the extent to which it could contribute to the *dissemination* of the innovation. Its activities were restricted to the conventional dissemination strategies of advertising and promotion – strategies effective in promoting sales, but not tailored to the particular characteristics of the innovation. Responsibility for designing a set of 'EEP-specific' dissemination strategies was also devolved to the state education officer level and shortcomings in negotiation resulted in the invoking of conventional systems strategies for disseminating the innovation more as a 'product' to be sold than as a set of problematic ideas – a situation which overlooked the potential disruption that the innovation might cause in the structures and practices of institutional settings.

For example, at the school administration level, the innovation encountered obstacles in the structure of conventional discipline structures. Distribution of the innovation materials was influenced by the habitual sorting patterns of administrators (principals, teacher-librarians), who tend to react to the steady inflow of curricular materials by categorising them according to 'subjects' – subjects which, like the curriculum committees which administer them, are discipline based. This specific example illustrates possibly the most fundamental problem confronting environmental education, for if the conventional curriculum is a jigsaw puzzle made up of subject 'pieces', then environmental education may be a piece of a different puzzle altogether.

Ironically, the structure of the EEP materials themselves contributed to their disciplinary tagging and hence conflicted with the interdisciplinary intent of the innovation. The primary school materials comprise four publications which contain a 'rhetoric of environmental education' and suggested practical activities. The rhetoric outlines four forms of environmental education – education *about, in, from* and *for* the environment. The first three are conventional forms, being concerned with the development of awareness, investigative skills and sensitivity to the environment in a way which does not challenge existing institutional structures and practices. The fourth – education *for* the environment – dictates environmentally and socially critical environmental education (concerned with the machinations of environmental decision making and problem solving). This is the project's stated preferred perspective. But the activities included in the four publications are more eclectic – two publications are clearly discipline-oriented and totally concerned with education *about* the environment. Further, these two publications *do not* include the project's preferred rhetoric in support of education *for* the environment, and, moreover, all four publications are *separately available*. Consequently, given the normal disciplinary structures in schools and the associated sorting procedures habitually used by administrators receiving ordered curriculum materials, it is to be expected that this type of publication, with its 'subject appeal', would be slotted into a disciplinary framework from the moment it arrived in the schools.

The structure of the materials is important because it provides an example of the way in which the innovation acts as a 'slogan system'. 'Environmental education' is defined tightly enough in the rhetoric in the project's main publication, *Environmental Education: A Sourcebook for Primary Education*, but the spirit of the reform is not realised in the 'practical activities' components of the materials, and sales data reveal that the main publication (and hence the project's rhetoric of environmental education) is not purchased by many of the schools using the materials. Thus, as a consequence of their structure, the EEP materials can be used in situations characterised, on the one hand, by education *about*, *in* and *from* the environment and, on the other, by the *absence* of education *for* the environment. The materials, and the name 'environmental education', are used to support education *about*, *in* and *from* the environment which is conventional in terms of its disciplinary structure, informational context, and teacher–pupil interactions. To interpret environmental education in this sense is to legitimate and continue the 'stable state' of existing educational structures and practices.

Thus the EEP is an Australian example of an attempt to disseminate information via a medium-level network (that is, one made up of educational consultants within the respective states) built around existing goals and institutions. However, the EEP is also an example of the deleterious effects of separtating *theory* (represented by the project's stated philosophical position on environmental education) from *practice* (represented in the accounts of existing environmental education programs). One outcome of this disjunction of theory and practice is that the project mediates a 'slogan system' in which the label of a potential reform can be used to describe and legitimate (and therefore to reproduce) existing practices.

An American example

The second example of tension and contradiction at the national level involves a recent sequence of events organised by the North American Association for Environmental Education. In August 1983, the association held its 'First National Congress for Environmental Education Futures: Policies and Practices' at the University of Vermont in Burlington, Vermont. One of its main objectives was to formulate a national policy which could guide environmental education in the United States of America for several years. At a workshop of the elementary-secondary section of the conference, a paper entitled 'The challenges of K–12 environmental education' (Hungerford 1983) was tabled with a view to providing some structure and impetus to the policy-making discussions. In 1984, substantially the same paper was published as one of three invited definitional papers 'outlining new directives and challenges in the field' (Sacks 1984, p.v) – it was the only paper which related to elementary and secondary education (Hungerford & Volk 1984).

In his original paper Hungerford begins by expressing concern about the state of environmental education, claiming that 'the year 1983 finds it, by and large, to be neither pervasive nor very persuasive in the USA' (Hungerford 1983, p. 3). He then identifies a number of challenges for environmental education. The first is 'accepting and focusing on the most appropriate goal for environmental education', which he suggests should be 'to provide an education which results in environmentally-affirmative citizenship', arguing that 'students must not only be knowledgeable about the environment, they must also have a set of skills which will permit them to function as change agents in society' (p. 4). In other words, Hungerford suggests that the 'ultimate goal' of environmental education should be understood as education *for* the environment rather than education *about* the environment. Having suggested 'the most appropriate goal', he claims that 'the ultimate goal of environmental education is either being ignored by practitioners or perceived as something that can be met through awareness education' (p. 4).

The second challenge identified by Hungerford (1983) is 'operationalizing environmental literacy: selecting appropriate goals'. He claims that educational research has been only partially effective in identifying those 'variables which influence behavior':

> Although researchers have investigated such variables as environmental sensitivity, knowledge of issues, beliefs, values, locus of control, and a number of population demographics, in none of the studies conducted thus far have they been able to account for a substantial amount of variance associated with behaviour in a manner that is generalizeable to large segments of the population overall. (p. 5)

His comments reflect an applied science (technocratic) view of educational research, where the educational context is seen as a system made up of discrete variables which influence behaviour in a 'generalizeable' way.

In a more prescriptive statement – one which suggests that the *type* of educational research itself is not being viewed as problematic – Hungerford says that: 'This is not to infer that said research is without merit – it is simply a matter of noting that a great deal remains to be done with respect to identifying variables or groups of variables which will predict behaviour' (p. 6).

Despite pointing to the shortcomings of educational research in environmental education and urging that more be done in the same vein, Hungerford does claim that 'enough evidence exists to guide us in generating goals for instructional decision-making which permit us to predict outcomes with a high degree of confidence' (p. 6) and that 'through this research, we have learned enough about environmental behaviour to be able to predict at least some of the elements which must be incorporated into instructional programs to make them successful' (p. 6). In the light of this research evidence, he recommends that a particular set of goals be accepted – 'we must begin somewhere' (p. 6). The set of goals he suggests the environmental education community accept is his own (see Hungerford, Peyton & Wilke 1981).

The third challenge identified by Hungerford is 'taking the goals to the classroom'. Having stressed the need for consensus on goals, he cites Volk, Hungerford and Tomera (1983) in posing five questions considered essential to addressing the issue of 'taking the goals to the classroom' (Hungerford 1983, p. 10):

1   To what extent is this goal important?
2   To what extent do existing curricula accomplish this goal?
3   To what extent is there a need for new curricula addressing this goal?
4   To what extent would new curricula addressing this goal be used by teachers?
5   To what extent would inservice teacher education be needed for new curricula addressing this goal?

Hungerford's acceptance that these are important questions about the realisation of his goals shows a technocratic perspective of innovation: the process of educational change is oriented towards goals; these goals are determined independently of practitioners; change is materials-mediated; and the notion of 'inservice' is accepted as unproblematic.

Hungerford places central importance on goals in his suggestions for improving environmental education: 'It seems obvious that unless developers of instructional materials and teacher trainers accept the goals and the research findings associated with the goals, not much will be accomplished' (p. 13).

A *power-coercive* model of change is mooted – one where change is imposed on the educational community by superordinate political-legislative systems: 'The easiest strategy [for convincing teacher educators that they must train teachers for environmental education] would be to make such training mandatory in every state in the USA' (p. 14). The only perceived alternative to power-coercive strategies is to 'hawk the goals and the need for their implementation at teacher educator conferences and to do so till the message is internalized' (p. 14). Beyond the 'hawking of goals', a form of competency-based education is prescribed: 'A major step in effecting this change [in teacher education] is the identification of those competencies needed by teachers which will enable them to become effective environmental instructors' (p. 14). A list of these competencies is referred to. They were prepared by the same authors as the goals statements (Wilke, Peyton & Hungerford 1980).

There is no doubt that Hungerford's technocratic approach to educational change is a common one that has a well-developed rationale in the literature and has served environmental education well in its efforts to develop a base of curriculum materials. But embedded in it is an obvious contradiction. Advocates of the technocratic approach, including Hungerford, criticise the propensity of developers and educators for educational decision-making that is 'intuitive' rather than 'empirical'.

> Unfortunately, both developers of curricula and professional educators have a propensity for making educational decisions on an intuitive rather than on an empirical basis . . . (Hungerford 1983, p. 13)

They also suggest that developers and teacher trainers (and therefore, presumably, teachers and students) accept *as given* the goals of environmental education determined by outsiders. However, these suggestions separate the 'theory' of the innovation (this remaining the province of outsiders) from the 'practice' (the work of practitioners), thus reducing the opportunity for practitioners to theorise about and research their own activities – to improve the rationality of their own practice – and thereby promoting decision-making that is 'intuitive'. To suggest power-coercive models of change and to speak of 'hawking the goals' until 'the message is internalized' (Hungerford 1983, p. 14) is to diminish the professional status of teachers to that of technicians who must accept on faith (that is, *intuitively*) the goals and embedded values of outside goal-setters.

Environmental education: Technocratised educational reform

These three examples show that the *organisation* of environmental education – its infrastructure and strategies for educational change – is predominantly managerial-hierarchical and technocratic in character. This form of organisation presupposes that curriculum materials, if properly prepared, can be effective change agents; that 'experts' can bring pre-existing, positive 'solutions' to classroom practitioners; that 'solutions' developed centrally have universal effectiveness; and that there is a 'passive' consumer at the end of a delivery system. As the American case shows, goals can be set, legislative or less power-coercive structures of 'persuasion' employed, teaching competencies determined and instrumental research and evaluation conducted – all with little or no recognition of, or attention to, the educational theories of practitioners in schools. Organisational responses to environmental education are based on a technocratic assumption: educational change is assumed to be *independent* of the differences between the beliefs and justifications of the social context in which the innovation is formulated and those of the social context in which the innovation is to be practised. The teacher's role is perceived as that of a technician implementing educational values determined by others, and failure of an innovation is accounted for in teacher-deficit terms. The comments of one writer show this attitude clearly:

> The writer observed long ago that there is a very real difference between establishing goals for instruction on one hand and seeing those goals implemented on the other. The reasons for this discrepancy are many and frustrating and will not be discussed here lest the writer be tempted to enter into a tirade of criticism on the educational community as a whole. (Hungerford 1983, p. 10)

And in a symposium on environmental education research at the North American Association for Environmental Education Annual Conference in 1982, it was claimed that research showed that:

> Teachers generally have good comprehension of what environmental education is and what its goals are, but however good these intentions, researchers and professionals have called into question the competence and ability of these teachers to accomplish the goals of environmental education. (Wilke & Leatherman 1982)

I will argue that teacher-deficit explanations of the failure of environmental education to meet its goals are ill-conceived—that the *presently dominant perspectives of educational change and research are responsible for structuring 'the innovation' in such a way that its operational form is incapable of meeting its socially and environmentally critical charter.* A managerial-hierarchical form of organisation, informed by an empiricist, objectivist epistemology, and adopting an RDDA or similarly depoliticised, technocratic view of educational change, far from being—as claimed by its supporters on the basis of its objectivist epistemology—a *neutral* administrative process, is itself political. Its politics are the politics of preservation of the *status quo*, of *reproduction*, in this case, of non-critical education *about* the environment. In brief, I will show that present perceptions of educational change create the conditions for stability in the face of change in environmental education.

Stability in the face of change
In Australia's Environmental Education Project (EEP), there are several illustrations of the potential of a technocratic view of educational change to reproduce itself. Perhaps the most fundamental is the very use of an RDDA-type materials development model. The model itself shares a managerial-hierarchical outlook: it assumes 'that a universal, logical and efficient procedure exists for the definition and organisation of change. It also suggests a neutrality to the change process itself: the problem of change is not to consider the moral or political structure of an institution but to implement a schema of order, precision and clarity' (Popkewitz 1983, p. 24). According to Popkewitz, one of the technocratic assumptions of the RDDA model is that 'the discourse of change can be treated independently of the institutional norms, beliefs and patterns in which the language is embedded' (p. 25). The EEP experience provides clear examples of this assumption. The use of a loose grouping of systems representatives to put into operation a pre-existing and independently negotiated reform concept appears to be based on the assumption that discourse about the reform concept can be continued from one context (the norms, beliefs and patterns of the central development agency) to another (those of the systems representatives). The use of dissemination strategies which treat the innovation as a product to be sold seems to be based on the same assumption—that

value differences between the setting in which the innovation is formulated (the central development agency) and the setting in which the innovation is implemented (schools) will not affect the reform effort. This assumption fails to take into account the educational problems that arise in particular settings, and therefore the institutional constraints which shape educational practices remain unaddressed and persist.

The pervasiveness and self-perpetuating quality of the technocratic worldview in institutional education are well illustrated when we consider interdisciplinarity in relation to environmental education in general and the EEP in particular. Among those involved in environmental education, there is a growing awareness that the excessive specialisation of analytic researchers has bred socially ignorant technicians – individuals who are unaware of the social and environmental implications of their work and are therefore ineffective agents in the resolution of (and perhaps even unwitting contributors to) a range of environmental problems. This specialisation is matched by educational fragmentation, characterised by discipline-oriented teaching and research (see Smolicz 1974). Environmental problems, however, mainly concern 'quality of life' issues – they have a perceived 'social need' component – and such problems cannot be resolved by applying any one discipline. In response to these perceptions, environmental education reformers stress the interdisciplinary nature of environmental education. Statements ranging in origin from the Belgrade Charter to the EEP include prescriptions for interdisciplinarity; the EEP's advocacy of education *for* the environment *via* an issues-oriented approach (see Womersley & Stokes 1981) is in line with Bernstein's claim that 'to accomplish any form of integration (as distinct from different subjects focusing upon a common problem, which gives rise to what could be called a *focused* curriculum) there must be some relational idea, a supra-content concept, which focuses upon general principles at a high level of abstraction' (Bernstein 1971, p. 60). The paradox is that the technocratic and managerial character of the RDDA-based project operations directs attention away from the dynamics of the implementation setting generally and particularly from the serious obstacles posed to interdisciplinary environmental education by disciplinary structures in schooling (as expressed, for example, in the prevalence of subject-oriented curricula) – structures which themselves are legitimated by technocratic thinking. Separately available EEP materials concerned exclusively with education *about*, *in* and *from* the environment invite only 'symbolic' reform, which reinforces the structures and epistemology which oppose environmental education.

Ironically, the beliefs and justifications embedded in the implementation setting tend to offer reciprocal support to the technocratic perspective of educational change. For example, the tendency for schools to make extensive use of *texts* (as written; as 'scripts for performance') reinforces the view that practical human problems (those of changing educational practices) can be solved by the application of a universally applicable set of 'solutions' embodied in the textual product of an administrative process ('decisions' or 'guidelines for action', for example). The discipline-centred curriculum implies a fragmentation of knowledge that is consistent with the specialised nature of technological processes in the wider community and, to the extent that environmental education is associated with the *science* discipline, an essentially technocratic scientific worldview is promoted. Habitual patterns of teaching treat the learner as a passive recipient of factual information and place the teacher in a position of authority (relative to the learner) regarding knowledge (Henry 1980), with administrative responsibilities for selecting and ordering the knowledge that is judged by the teacher to be worthwhile. Further, teachers possess definite views of teaching and curriculum which influence their actions (see, for example, Elliot & Adelman 1976; Henry 1981b). These presuppositions usually include a view of knowledge as objective, value-free and divided into disciplines, and a view of teaching as the didactic imparting of factual information (Robottom 1984). The readiness of school administrators and practitioners to accept a curriculum from outside is an acknowledgement of their willingness to adopt the role of recipients in a technological process – to act as subordinate implementers, or 'mere operatives or consumers' (UNESCO 1980, p. 26). These presuppositions combine with the structural features of the implementation setting (subjects, timetables, specialist teachers) to sustain a technocratic perspective.

In environmental education, there is a *symbiotic relationship* in which conventional approaches to professional development and the characteristics of the context where change is intended interact to foster the interpretation of environmental education as education *about* the environment. Such an interpretation legitimates the maintenance of existing organisational, teaching and curriculum patterns. There is a dynamic, self-reinforcing relationship between the dominant perspective of innovation (as expressed in materials development and dissemination), institutional characteristics (patterns of teaching and curriculum) and a particular (technocratic) interpretation of the innovation itself. In environmental education, this relationship is such that any factor which supports either education *about* the environment *or* existing patterns of organisation, teaching or curriculum maintains the symbiotic balance of the interaction. This symbiotic balance may be understood as a dynamic *stability in the face of change*.

'Environmental education' as a slogan system
One factor maintaining this dynamic stability in the face of change is the generic (and perhaps ambiguous) nature of the term 'environmental education'. Environmental education has been defined in three ways: 'education *in* the environment', 'education *about* the environment' and 'education *for* the environment' (see Lucas 1979). The first two definitions enable the notion of 'environmental education' to act as a *slogan system*. Certain environment-related activities are used – and environmental education is said to be happening *because* these activities are taking place – in teaching–learning situations that are conventional in their disciplinary structure, information content and teacher–student interactions. These activities are considered environmentally *educational* (their affinity with existing educational structures and practices fosters this interpretation); they are, however, not distinctively *environmental* education in the sense of education *for* the environment. Of the three definitions, 'education *about* the environment' is far more readily assimilated into existing structures and practices than 'education *for* the environment'. The generic nature of the term 'environmental education' leaves open the question of what will actually happen under the slogan (*in*, *about*, or *for*) and thus permits, if not encourages, change that is *symbolic* only.

Such a slogan system has several alleged benefits: the repertoire of candidate activities for existing disciplinary (usually science) programs is increased; environment-related activities are used; timetabling problems are avoided; habitual teaching patterns are not threatened; and the 'host' program gains from whatever status and added attraction to funding bodies the label 'environmental education' carries. But to teach environmental education as education *about* the environment constitutes a change that is largely *symbolic* – at best representing a quantitative increase in the amount of environment-related work – and reinforces such institutional characteristics as the subject basis of the curriculum and didactic teaching. The problem is that these characteristics act as barriers to the qualitative change defined as 'education *for* the environment': the generic nature of the term 'environmental education' becomes part of the problem that proponents of environmental education as an educational reform must address.

In the next section, these issues in the specific reform effort of environmental education are considered in the broader context of theories of curriculum reproduction and transformation.

Reproduction and transformation

Thomas Popkewitz (1983) presents a view of educational change which draws attention to the ideological character of schooling. He claims that beneath the surface layers of teaching and curriculum practice and structures there are underlying principles of legitimacy, authority and social order – a deeper ideology. If we apply his perspective to the current discussion, it can be said that environmental education *reproduces*, rather than transforms, the 'surface layers' of teaching and curriculum. But what is being reproduced when environmental education is interpreted as education *about* the environment runs deeper than the visible 'surface layer' of structures (discipline-based subjects) and practices (conventional didactic teaching) in institutional education. As Popkewitz points out, it is an entire *view of knowledge and of social order* that is being reproduced.

The view of knowledge being reproduced in the dynamic relationship between the dominant perspective of the innovation process, institutional characteristics and the innovation itself is essentially *technocratic* and has parallels in the distinguishing features of accepted conceptions of science. These features are:

1 *Rationality*: the assumption that there is only one rational method by which all problems can be solved. This notion further assumes that the nature of reality in the problem-solving context is known and understood, and that events are predictable. This assumption is reinforced by a view of innovation which fails to acknowledge the existence and influence of the norms, beliefs and patterns of the institution where educational change is being sought. The accepted 'rational method' of science – advancement by empirical refutation of widely published and criticised truth-claims – is reinforced by the tendency of environmental education as education *about* the environment to be accommodated in the structure of conventional *science* education.

2 *Objectivity*: the assumption that the only true understanding of a problem is one expressed in terms of factual information. The implication of the empiricist models of knowledge is that scientific knowledge, by virtue of the rigour of the rational method of its generation, is separable from, and has primacy over, such 'metaphysical' matters as human values and interests. This notion too is reinforced by conventional views of innovation which fail to recognise the different sets of values in the implementation setting, and by the association of environmental education with the 'science' subject in the curriculum. The importance of factual information to the understanding of problems is reinforced by didactic methods of teaching which stress the value of imparted information.

3 *Truth*: the proposition that for every genuine question there is only one true answer. This follows from the conception of a scientific community as an 'open society' in which proffered truth-claims receive widespread criticism. The notion of 'truth' is consistent with the view that empirical refutation of old theories is followed by the formulation of new ones in a progressive march away from uncertainty. In the case

of environmental education, the 'one true answer' assumption is interpreted as 'only *one* solution exists for each environmental problem' – an interpretation reinforced by the tendency in science education to stress technical (rather than, for example, practical) solutions to problems, and by didactic teaching patterns which establish *teachers'* solutions as the only ones of consequence. The view of innovation which implies the *universal* applicability of centrally produced curriculum materials (as solutions to the problems teachers wrestle with in environmental education) also supports this assumption.

The view of social order reproduced by the three-way relationship between the dominant perspective of innovation as a process, existing institutional patterns and a technocratic interpretation of the innovation is closely tied to the epistemological considerations expressed earlier. The learner's context is one in which knowledge is fragmented, selected and sequenced by other individuals 'in authority'. The teachers are authorities not only in knowledge, but usually in school and classroom management as well. The learner is treated as a relatively passive, receptive individual whose knowledge and perspectives are shaped over time by the authority figure; that is, the individual is denied the role of actor in the creation of history and culture. This view of social order is antipathetic to the learning autonomy and responsibility sought in education *for* the environment.

Technocratisation: Countering the critical aims of environmental education

In a recent article, Kemmis criticises the 'technologisation of our thought – our willingness to subjugate our human, convivial intelligence and capacity for critical thought to technologies of reason'. His concern echoes Buzzati-Traverso's warning which was quoted at the beginning of this essay. Kemmis claims that:

> In a world dominated by contending specialisms, arcane technologies and the proliferation of mass solutions to practical problems, we seem all too ready to give up our own critical intelligence and to accept as the solutions to our own problems the forms of life fashioned for us by others – where those 'others' are 'experts', 'specialists' or . . . 'the technologists of reason'. (Kemmis 1987, ch. 7.2, p. 1)

I have argued that environmental education is being systematically 'technocratised' to the point where its operational form fails to meet its socially and environmentally critical charter. I further contend that the presently dominant technocratic perspective of innovation which underpins the organisation and shapes the infrastructure of environmental education is part of the machinery that supports this 'technocratisation' and thus undermines the critical aspirations of environmental education.

By conserving and reproducing a technocratic view of the world – one centred on rationality, objectivity, truth and control – environmental education as education *about* the environment creates the impression that environmental problems are susceptible to resolution through technical, applied science means. Based on such elements as fragmentation (through a division of knowledge into specialisms manifested in a division of labour between specialists and non-specialists), means–end thinking, eradication of values and large-scale administrative and financial support, it promotes the view that there exists a 'logic of issues resolution'. The impression is that, given sufficient time and knowledge about an environmental issue, an appropriate course of action will emerge and the best solution will be discovered. And furthermore, these deeper and 'hidden' impressions interact with more tangible institutional constraints and result in teachers and students rarely progressing from an 'awareness development' phase to the 'action' or participation phase prescribed in the accepted guiding principles of environmental education.

The technocratic worldview promoted by education *about* the environment ignores the important qualitative dimensions of the majority of environmental issues which involve 'quality of life' or 'social need' concerns—emotions, beliefs, aspirations, aesthetics and, perhaps most important of all, vested interests. It could be argued that a view of the resolution of environmental problems that stresses the role of technical 'machinery' (i.e. the processes of an objective, applied science method) creates a false impression of the way these issues are resolved by masking such value-laden political machinations as negotiation, manoeuvring, persuasion, the offering of inducements, the exertion of influence, and so on. This false impression of the decision-making processes involved in the resolution of environmental problems creates the conditions for the intrusion of *unaccounted vested interests* in those processes—conditions which increase the risk of excessive exploitation of the environment.

This section has focused on the organisation and infrastructure of environmental education. Two main propositions have been advanced.

The first is that the dominant perspective of innovation in environmental education is technocratic. It interacts with institutional characteristics and popular interpretations of environmental education to form a hegemony, confronting attempts at educational reform with a dynamic stability in the face of change. This hegemony is hostile to environmentally and socially critical environmental education. Organisational strategies based on the dominant view of innovation amount to a means of 'control' over practitioners, who as a consequence lack the autonomy and responsibility to challenge the dynamic stability which opposes environmental education as education *for* the environment.

The second proposition is that in addition to continuing the 'surface features' of institutional structures and practices, the dominant perspective of innovation in environmental education reproduces an entire view of knowledge and of social order. While assuming the trappings of neutrality by its objectivist epistemology, it reproduces rather than transforms the social conditions which pose threats to both the environment and the forms of education which preserve rather than challenge critical consciousness about environmental problems.

The present analysis suggests that this technocratic approach is not the only—or even the best—approach to improving environmental education. The next section suggests an alternative approach to professional development in environmental education.

An alternative approach to professional development in environmental education

The previous section suggested that the way in which environmental education is organised contributes to the conflict between the aims of environmental education on the one hand and the practice of environmental education in schools on the other. The organisation of environmental education not only is inconsistent with the rhetoric of education *for* the environment, but—despite the reformist zeal of education *for* the environment—reinforces the reproductive character of schooling. Rationalist, tech-

nocratic organisational approaches, conventional didactic teaching and disciplinary curriculum practices, and interpretations of environmental education as education *about*
the environment, seem to reinforce each other in a way which resists authentic educational reform and contributes to the continuity of an 'education *about* the environment' form of environmental education.

The main challenge for environmental education today is to recognise and find
an alternative to the existing technocratic organisation of professional development in
environmental education. Professional development in environmental education needs
to be seen as problematic and amenable to change.

A conventional construction of the problem of professional development in environmental education

In conventional (RDDA-type) perspectives of educational reform, the problem of professional development in environmental education is construed as a 'rhetoric–reality gap'.
The 'rhetoric' is the language or theory of the academy–the policy statements validated by educational researchers and legitimised at international conferences (originally at Belgrade and Tbilisi)–and the 'reality' is the educational practices of teachers
in schools. The appropriateness of the RDDA form of organisation is taken for granted:
the subversive role of organisational strategies in aiding and abetting the continuity
of existing processes and structures is not recognised. Conventional instrumental
research tackles the problem of how to bring the practice of teachers into line with
the theory of the academy. Actions are based on the empiricist-objectivist assumption
that research findings represent a type of knowledge that can be applied by teachers
as 'solutions' at other sites. 'Educational theory' resides in the language of researchers
in the academy; teachers are 'atheoretical', and their activities are purely practical. The
logical conclusion is that practitioners are considered unwilling or unable to understand or translate into practice the findings of researchers; that is, conventional (RDDA-
type) perspectives of educational reform result in deficit theories of teachers.

This view of the problem of professional development in environmental education
is incapable of offering a sensible account of the tensions and contradictions within
the infrastructure of the environmental education movement.

A reconstruction of the problem of professional development in environmental education

Underpinning a reconstruction of the problem of professional development in environmental education is the proposition that practitioners–far from being 'atheoretical' in
the way assumed by technocratic RDDA-type approaches to the improvement of the
organisation of environmental education, actually have theoretical views which guide
their practice.

Carr contends that 'it is difficult to know how any teacher could ever undertake
any educational practice without some knowledge and understanding of the situation
in which he is operating and some idea of what it is that needs to be done' (Carr 1983,
p. 12). In his view, 'everyone engaged in educational pursuits . . . must already have
some "educational theory" in terms of which their activities are structured and their
decisions are made' (p. 12). This interactionist view of the relationship between theory
and practice is quite different from the RDDA view that theory is the domain of the
researcher and practice the domain of the teacher. Carr believes that:

> It is. . . somewhat misguided to regard research and teaching as, respectively, the 'theory'

and the 'practice' of education. They are both theory-guided practices, each of which may
be undertaken with varying degrees of intelligence and success. The twin assumptions
that educational research is non-practical and educational practice is non-theoretical are,
therefore, entirely misleading. All practices have 'theory' embedded in them and this is
just as true for the practice of 'theoretical' pursuits like educational research as it is for
practical pursuits like teaching. Teachers could no more teach without thinking (and hence
'theorising') about what they are doing than researchers could produce educational theories
without engaging in the sort of practices distinctive to their activity. (Carr 1983, p. 12)

According to Carr, the conventional view of the problem of professional development distorts the relationship of theory and practice in three ways:

> [Firstly,] to regard theory–practice gaps as problems of 'communication' or 'implementa-
> tion' that are peculiar to practical activities like education, distorts the fact that a gap between
> theory and practice is the kind of difficulty that can also occur in the course of any theo-
> retical undertaking. Secondly, the assumption that these difficulties can somehow be
> identified and tackled 'in theory' and then 'applied' in practice tends to conceal how they
> are, in fact, generated out of the experience of practitioners and only emerge when the
> way in which these experiences are usually organised is found to be ineffective. Thirdly,
> the view that the problems that these gaps create can be overcome by converting theo-
> retical knowledge into rules of action overlooks the simple point that gaps between theory
> and practice, whether they occur for researchers or teachers, are closed by the practitioners
> themselves formulating decisions in the light of the framework of understanding that they
> already possess. (Carr 1983, pp. 13–14)

Carr's perspective of theory and practice may be summarised as follows (Robottom
1987, p. 79):

- educational problems (e.g. the improvement of environmental education) are constituted
  of gaps between theory and practice;
- *everyone* (teachers, consultants researchers, materials developers) engaged in educational
  pursuits possesses an educational theory;
- *anyone* engaged in educational pursuits may therefore experience the difficulties of a
  theory–practice gap;
- theory–practice gaps – and the educational problems they constitute – only emerge from
  the experiences of practitioners;
- equally, theory–practice gaps can be closed only by practitioners themselves – through
  a process of critical appraisal of the respective adequacies of their own educational
  practices and their own educational theories.

Given this perspective of theory and practice, the conventional way of looking at
the issue of professional development in environmental education – a discrepancy
between international language and local classroom practice – is dangerously misleading.
It is misleading because it fails to recognise that *everyone* engaged in educational pursuits
possesses an educational theory and thereby overlooks the possibility of the existence
of theory–practice gaps *within* the activities of international conferences, national curriculum projects and school programs. It is dangerous because it fails to countenance
the possibility of subversive contradictions in the settings in which environmental education is practised.

If we accept the relationship between theory and practice outlined by Carr, it
becomes possible to offer an alternative view of the issue of professional development
in environmental education. The issue can be seen as a series of theory–practice gaps
at *all levels* of environmental education activities, rather than simply an inability of

practitioners to translate the theory of the (international) academy into (classroom) practice. Given Carr's perception of the relationship between theory and practice, professional development in environmental education is 'professional' if the 'theory' it refers to is the theory (beliefs and assumptions) in terms of which *individual practitioners* understand their environmental educational practice (i.e. their own professional work). And there is scope for 'development' if there are discrepancies between personal theory and professional practice, or between these and the physical or social structure and social relationships of the setting in which environmental educational practices occur. The issue of professional development in environmental education, then, is the persistence of professional theory–practice gaps at all levels environmental education activities, that is, there is continuing 'irrationality' as a result of a lack of conscious, critical self-appraisal of 'the adequacy of the concepts, beliefs, assumptions, and values incorporated in prevailing theories of educational practice' (Carr 1983, p. 14).

At the beginning of this essay, several excerpts from UNESCO documents warned that the rationality (or 'critical intelligence') of practitioners in the environmental education movement can be overridden when the 'solutions' of outside experts are proffered and accepted in technocratic forms of organisation. The conventional, technocratic organisation of environmental education takes for granted the worth or appropriateness of particular educational ends or the values intrinsic to educational processes and practices and thereby weakens the ability of practitioners to appraise their theories and practices and contributes to irrationality. In the case of environmental education, continued irrationality maintains a dynamic stability in the face of change.

If the issue of professional development in environmental education is reconstructed and viewed in a way which emphasises the relationship between theory and practice at all levels, some pointers emerge to the kind of activities that might succeed in achieving sustained improvement in educational practices in general and in environmental education in particular. In the words of Carr:

> If . . . it is recognised that there is nothing to which the phase 'educational theory' can coherently refer other than to the theory that actually guides educational practices, then it becomes apparent that a theoretical activity explicitly concerned to influence educational practice can only do so if it influences the 'theory' in terms of which these practices are made intelligible. 'Educational theory', on this view, is not an 'applied theory' that 'draws on' theories from philosophy and the social sciences, but rather refers to the whole enterprise of critically appraising the adequacy of the concepts, beliefs, assumptions and values incorporated in prevailing theories of educational practice. This does not mean that the relationship of theory to practice is such that theory 'implies' practice, or is 'derived' from practice or even 'reflects' practice. Rather, by subjecting the beliefs and justifications of existing and ongoing practical traditions to rational criticism, theory transforms practice by transforming the ways in which practice is experienced and understood. The transition is not, therefore, from theory to practice as such, but rather from irrationality to rationality, from ignorance and habit to knowledge and reflection. (Carr 1983, p. 14)

The interpretation of 'educational theory' as rational criticism of the dialectic of theory and practice is consistent with the nature of the issue of professional development in environmental education. The epistemology of this interpretation of educational theory is interactionist: it sees knowledge as an interplay of the individual's subjective views on the one hand and the social, cultural, historical and environmental context in which the individual lives on the other. Environmental education knowledge, then, is an interplay of the theories that guide the practitioner's environmental education actions on one the hand and institutional structures and relationships on the other.

Appraisal of such theory and practice is *emancipatory* since it frees people from the 'mystification of ideology, the dictates of habit and precedent, or the compulsions of self-interested authorities' (Kemmis 1987, p. 26). In the case of environmental education, such appraisal may be a way of overcoming the tendency for the practices of environmental education to promote continuity (or at best, quantitative change) rather than authentic qualitative improvement.

In attempting to reinterpret the issue of professional development in environmental education, I have proposed that:

- The present organisation of environmental education, although exhibiting examples of tension and contradiction, also illustrates *continuity of educational practice* – a continuity maintained by the 'technocratising' influence of existing forms of organisation.

- Conventional perceptions of this situation are in terms of a large-scale theory–practice gap, where the 'theory' is the language and policy of the international academy and the 'practice' is what goes on in the classroom. This is a distorted view of the relationship between theory and practice, which diverts attention from the way in which environmental education is organised and diminishes the need for practitioners to exercise their critical intelligence. The result is that the innovation is 'technocratised'.

- An alternative view is that environmental education suffers from a series of theory–practice gaps at *all* levels, where 'theory' is the set of beliefs and assumptions that are held by individual practitioners and in terms of which they understand their educational practice. The problem of professional development exists because these theory–practice gaps exist; the problem continues because these theory–practice gaps *exist unacknowledged* within the organisational infrastructure of environmental education. They are at once maintained and denied by a distorted view of 'educational theory'.

- An alternative interpretation of 'educational theorising' sees it as rational criticism (by those engaged in educational pursuits) of the relationship between theory, practice and circumstance. The dialectical epistemology of this interpretation of educational theory acknowledges practitioners' interpretive categories and the interactive relationship of these categories on the one hand, and personal and institutional practices on the other. By encouraging criticism, this interpretation of educational theory is emancipatory. Educational theorising opposes technocratisation.

In the light of these points, the *research* question of how to improve environmental education (or how to solve the problem of professional development in environmental education) becomes a question of how to improve educational theorising in environmental education. The next section addresses this issue.

Qualities of an adequate form of professional development in environmental education

Professional development in environmental education must be based on a form of educational inquiry that encourages a critical analysis of theories, practices and settings. Such an educational inquiry must possess at least two qualities:

- it must recognise the theories of practitioners of environmental education – their 'presuppositions about curriculum and teaching practice' (Robottom 1984, p. 12).

- it must acknowledge that the educational problem of environmental education involves not only discrepancies between the theory and the practice of individuals ('false consciousness'), but also discrepancies between individual theory and practice on the one hand, and social structures and relations on the other (oppression or hegemony). It must provide a means for closing both individual theory–practice gaps and the theory–practice gaps between individuals and social structures and relations. It must adopt a politicised view of environmental education and concern itself with educational theorising as *ideology critique*, recognising ideology in its various forms – false consciousness, oppression or hegemony.

I will argue that *action research* is a form of educational inquiry which possesses these qualities and is therefore an appropriate inquiry base for professional development in environmental education.

Action research: An appropriate inquiry base for professional development in environmental education?

Definition of action research

Action research is a form of self-reflective inquiry undertaken by participants in social (including educational) situations in order to improve the rationality and justice of (1) their own social or educational practices, (2) their understanding of these practices, and (3) the situations in which the practices are carried out (Kemmis 1982).

The method of action research

Action research acknowledges that teaching, and educational practice in general, is complex, problematic and uncertain, and takes place in a context which is equally complex, changeable and politically shaped. Its method involves recurrent cycles of three phases. There is a *planning* phase, in which existing professional activities are regarded as subject to change – individual practitioners look for 'dissatisfactions', areas with room for improvement, in their own professional activities. Of course, 'dissatisfactions' and 'improvement' are subjective terms – their meaning depends on the context in which they are used. In the *planning* phase, an educational activity is identified in which improvement is deemed possible. In the *action* phase, the plan is put into practice in an educational setting. In addition to trying to improve an educational activity, the practitioner organises a means of *monitoring* the process (for example, the activity may be videotaped or audiotaped). Ideally, the means of monitoring should be capable of detecting an improvement (in the practitioner's own terms) when it occurs. In the third phase, *reflection*, information collected during the monitoring phase is examined and analysed. In particular, practitioners reflect critically on the relationship between their practice (the monitored action) and their subjective view of what is being practised (the personal 'theory' that guides their practice).

> They may ask such questions as: 'Was improvement evident?' 'Did it go far enough?' 'What further changes to my practice might enable further improvement?' 'What institutional barriers were encountered in this attempt at improvement?' 'What beliefs and assumptions about teaching, schooling, or what is being taught were evident in my practice?' 'Is my conception of the innovation (my theory) in need of adjustment in light of this practical experience?' (Robottom 1985, p. 33)

In the light of the results of this three-phase action research cycle, the next *planning* phase is entered.

Action research, then, is mediated by *praxis*, by practitioners' critical reflection upon their professional activities. It aims at *personal* improvement through praxis applied to the dialectic between thought and action. It also aims at program and institutional improvement through praxis applied to the dialectic between individual action and societal structure and history (that of the program, or the institution, or society at large). Action research promotes rational decision making in the sense that the practitioner (or group of practitioners) is able to choose between alternative courses of professional action, the respective rationales of which have been subject to deliberation by the practitioners themselves.

The recurrent cycles of the three phases form the *action research spiral*, in which the knowledge from one cycle informs the strategic action of the next cycle. This process is illustrated in Figure 1.

Figure 1
The action research spiral

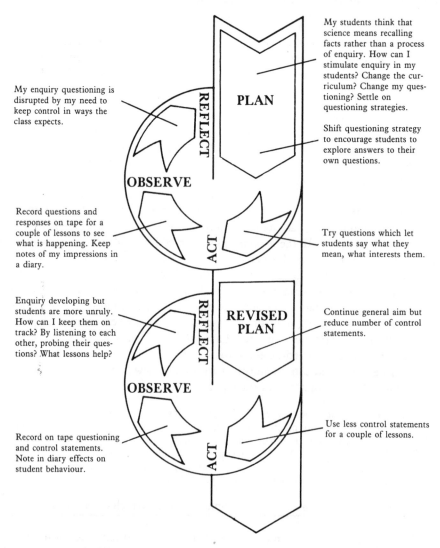

Source: S. Kemmis & R. McTaggart, *The Action Research Planner* (ECT432/732 *Action Research in Curriculum*) Deakin University, Vic., 1982, p. 11.

It is the action research *spiral* of successive cycles, rather than a single cycle of three phases (planning, action and reflection) that allows improvement in the rationality and justice of the practice itself, of the practitioners' understanding of the practice and of the practitioners' understanding of the situation in which the practices are carried out. Improvements perceived through 'trying out' some of the range of alternative actions point to further modifications and investigation. Only through a related series of action research cycles which apply the practitioner's own self-reflection to the self-reflective work of professional colleagues can the practitioner gain a measure of collaborative self-control in professional development. In the action research spiral, it is the individual's (or the group's) control over, and rationality in, personal and professional practice that is escalating; the medium is the series of action research cycles.

Information about practice is assembled during the monitoring phase of action research cycles. Brown (1981) suggests a number of means by which teachers engaging in action research may gather data to act as a basis for self-reflection, including open-ended questionnaires, diaries, lesson notes, minutes of meetings, 'case studies' of individual students, tape-recordings of lessons and 'structured observation' by an outside observer.

Structured observation by peers is facilitated in group- (or cluster-) based action research (Henry et al. 1981). In this form of action research, practitioners from different settings are drawn together because of similar curriculum or research interests, and they function as *self-critical communities*. As stated by Henry (1981a), group-based action research is characterised by the development of a project perspective on a problem shared by a group of practitioners; an awareness of the value of existing practice through the pooling of experiences; a commitment to self-reflection; and the development of skills in systematically monitoring practice and change. The functions of the 'critical community' of an action research group include co-operation in monitoring and description of practice, and discussion and analysis of issues and problems of mutual interest.

Action research as an inquiry base for professional development in environmental education

Action research is not distinguished from other forms of educational research by the means used to assemble data, but by its method of recurrent cycles of planning, action and reflection, and (more importantly) by its political theory. The political theory informing action research differs from that informing other educational research in its view of the 'phenomena' under study; its emphasis on participation and reflection; and its critique of ideology. I propose that this political theory matches the qualities necessary for an adequate inquiry base for professional development in environmental education.

The view of the 'phenomena' under study in action research

The term 'phenomena' is quoted to indicate that while we are concerned with action research's analogue of the particulate matter which forms the object of physical science and the organic matter which forms the object of biological science, the sense in which the term is used in action research is different from the conventional one. In physical and biological science, the objects of research are assumed to exist independently or 'objectively'. The 'phenomena' of action research, however, are *educational practices* — practical human actions taken by practitioners in the process of education. They do not exist independently of the researchers. In action research, these practices are studied by their practitioners with a view to professional improvement and the resolution of contradictions in their professional lives.

The actions or practices that form the 'phenomena' of action research are also regarded differently from the phenomena of applied sciences like human ethology. While dealing with the activities of humans, ethology treats such activities as *behaviours* capable of being studied in the same objective fashion as particles and organisms – as *determined* (for example, as responses to sets of stimuli). But the notion of activities as determined responses to stimuli directs the researcher's attention away from the interpretive categories (intentions, justifications and rationality) of the actor.

The 'actions' of action research are viewed in a more complex fashion. The activities of practitioners are regarded as *praxis*: action formed and directed by intentions, justifications and commitments. Action research directs the researchers' attention to the rationality of the actor (practitioner). 'Action' is seen as a contingent component in a dialectical relationship with the practitioner's theory (in terms of which the practitioner views the action as *educational*). In this dialectical relationship, actions are informed by the practitioner's theory (that is, the nature of prospective action is suggested by the theory), and actions inform the theory retrospectively (that is, the theory is modified in the light of the experience of the action). Actions are a test of theory as much as they issue from theory. The interpretive categories of practitioners are therefore central to action research. Thus action research complies with the first required quality of an appropriate form of educational inquiry for professional development in environmental education.

However, the dialectic in which action is a contingent component is a *double* one. Actions are also dialectically related to the *context of action*. Actions and practitioners' self-understandings are constrained and shaped by the limits imposed and the opportunities provided by the structure of the setting in which they occur, and actions are a test of the extent to and the ways in which the practitioner can shape the structure of that setting. Recognition of this second dialectic brings the social reality of the educational context into the ambit of action research.

This double dialectic, implicit in the notion of 'action' in action research, is diametrically opposed to the positivist notions of objectivity, independence and determinism implicit in conventional research terms such as 'phenomena', 'objects', 'organisms', 'variables', 'treatments' and 'behaviours'. Understanding the human actions of educational practice requires an exploration of both the subjective justifications and meanings of those actions and the practitioner–context relationship which constrains them. The dialectical view of 'action' that is embodied in action research is consistent with the need to recognise the way environmental education practices are shaped and constrained by both practitioners' theories and institutional structures and relationships.

Participation and reflection in action research

Only practitioners can explore this double dialectic. Only practitioners are privy to the theories which guide their own actions, and only practitioners can explore the limits and opportunities of their situation. While outsiders can assist with the development of descriptive accounts of practice (they can become facilitators), they come to the setting with their own theoretical perspectives – the practitioner must be involved if the relationship between private theory and personal practice is to be balanced. If the interpretive categories of the practitioner are not being represented, action research is not occurring.

The relationship between practitioner-researcher and any outsider involved in the action research is crucial. It is common for 'facilitators' to be involved in organising meetings of participants; contributing to a developing pool of curriculum materials and teaching ideas; providing monitoring assistance (e.g. audio-cassette recorders, typing of transcripts of tape-recorded lessons); and providing emotional and intellectual support to participants.

However, the very acts of providing assistance, such as curriculum materials and ideas, may be pre-emptive. These acts may forestall attempts by practitioners to scrutinise their own prior perspectives of curriculum (that is, to explain their own 'theory'). The provision of curriculum materials and ideas may impose the facilitators' theories – as manifested in the materials provided – upon practitioners. Such assistance may, from the outset, begin to create dependence of practitioners upon facilitators, and dependence may in turn interfere with the attainment of the 'symmetrical communications' which are so important to the notion of a 'critical community' that is built into group-based action research.

In action research, the *locus of control must remain internal*. The practitioner is the researcher: it is the practitioner who proposes the 'hypothesis' (that improvement is possible in an aspect of personal professional practice), who empirically 'tests the hypothesis' through his or her own practice, who engages in group deliberation about the relationship of theory and practice, and whose decision it is to act in certain changed ways as a result of that deliberation. By themselves conducting the research, the practitioners gain a better understanding of, and hence personal and collaborative control over, their own practices. The outcomes – a better understanding of personal practice and its justifications and of the possibilities for and limitations to improvement offered and imposed by the institutional context – are grounded in personal praxis and are therefore 'owned' by the practitioner and the participant group. In educational research based on action research, access to and release of information is controlled by practitioners. 'Ownership' and the internal 'locus of control' may need to be protected by a commitment on the part of all participants to a set of negotiated 'principles of procedure' which govern the research (for example, see Kemmis & Robottom 1981). Participation and 'ownership' by practitioners are essential to professional development in environmental education if the 'social control' potential of technocratic approaches is to be negated.

Ideology critique

In the discussion so far, I have concentrated on the concern of action research with an exploration of practitioners' theories and of the relationship between these theories and practitioners' practice. But action research is equally concerned with the other half of the double dialectic – the relationship between the power relations in the settings of practitioners' work on the one hand, and the nature of practitioners' understanding of their personal practice on the other. Action research aims not only to encourage practitioners to reflect on the relationship between their own theory and practice, but also to engage practitioners in inquiries into the ways in which their professional lives are determined by the structures and organisation of the situations in which they find themselves (for example, the historical and social conditions of institutional schooling). A fundamental characteristic of action research, then, is *ideology critique*, which

> ... is aimed at revealing to individuals how their beliefs and attitudes may be ideological illusions that help to preserve a social order which is alien to their collective experiences and needs. By demonstrating how ideological forces generate erroneous self-understandings, ideology critique aims to reveal their deceptive nature and so strip them of their power. (Carr & Kemmis 1983, p. 137)

It is clear that action research, which seeks to create the conditions for ideology critique, serves an *emancipatory* knowledge-constitutive interest. It aims to involve practitioners in inquiries that that will free them from 'the dictates of irrational or unjust habits, customs, precedents, coercion, or bureaucratic systematisation' (Carr & Kemmis 1983, p. 175). This aspect of the political theory of action research matches the crucial second quality of an appropriate form of educational inquiry for professional development in environmental education.

Summary: Guiding principles for professional development in environmental education

It has been argued that action research is an appropriate inquiry base for professional development in environmental education. If based on an action research perspective, professional development in environmental education would be committed to the following principles (Robottom 1987, pp. 80–3)[7]:

1 Professional development in environmental education should be *enquiry-based*.

Professional development activities in environmental education should encourage participants at all levels to adopt a research stance to their own environmental education practices. Current practices in environmental education (teaching, curriculum development, inservice activities, teacher education activities, institutional organisation. . .) should be regarded as problematic – as having the potential for improvement through participant research.

2 Professional development in environmental education should be *participatory and practice-based*.

Environmental education practices are shaped (guided or constrained) by the theories of practitioners themselves, and by the theories of others built into the structures and relationships of the institutions within which practitioners work. Environmental education problems are matters concerning the practices of individuals and groups: they occur when there are gaps between what practitioners think they are doing and what they are actually doing (these are problems of 'false consciousness'); and they occur when there are gaps between what they want to do and what they are actually able to do in their particular setting (these are problems of 'institutional pressure'). In either case, it is essential that the practitioner be directly involved in addressing these problems, because what is to count as a 'solution' will only become clear through a process of working through the relationship of theory and practice. Professional development courses consisting solely of prior 'training in the disciplines' conducted outside the work contexts of practitioners are of limited help in resolving these practical problems. Approaches to professional development that impose a division of labour between 'practitioners' and 'researchers' should be abandoned.

3 Professional development in environmental education should be *critical*.

Professional development in environmental education should entail a critique of the environmental and educational values and assumptions that inform existing environmental education policies, activities and organisational practices. It is through processes of enlightenment about the values informing and justifying policies, activities and organisational practices that change in these registers is made possible as practitioners come to an understanding of the field through their critical enquiries and develop their own theories about environment and education.

4 Professional development in environmental education should be *community-based*.

Environmental education problems are doubly idiosyncratic: the *environmental* issues that form the substance of environmental education work are usually specific in terms of time and space (this is simply to say that environmental conditions in different parts of the world are different); and *educational* problems are rarely susceptible to universal solutions (this is to say that the ecology of classrooms differs from classroom to classroom).

5 Professional development in environmental education should be *collaborative*.

There are two reasons for collaborative work in professional development in environmental education. Firstly, recognition of instances of false consciousness or institutional pressure often requires the assistance of colleagues working in similar circumstances (several heads are better than one). And secondly, many of the forces acting against improvement in environmental education are political in character, and collective action is usually more productive than individual efforts in the context of political struggles. (Examples of the political character of the forces shaping environmental education are: the tendency of schools (and governments) to favor a 'safe' form of environmental education like the teaching of basic ecological principles rather than the investigation of controversial local environmental issues; the tendency of textbook agents and educational consultants to favor the teaching of substantive content (information about the environment) rather than to encourage a critical, enquiry-based form of environmental education – because to do otherwise would be to threaten the relevance of their own expertise; the struggle for resources engaged in by interdisciplinary subject-based curriculum).

Notes

1 This essay is a development of a paper presented at the Third National Environmental Education Seminar and Workshops, Canberra, February 1987.

2 Hereafter referred to as the UNESCO program.

3 Professor William Stapp, former head of the UNESCO Secretariat in Environmental Education in Paris, traces the origins of the nature study and outdoor education movements to the liberal-progressive educational philosophies of Dewey, Whitehead, Rugg, Counts, and Parker from 1900–1940 (see Stapp 1982).

4 The 'trend papers' discussed at the workshops were later published (see UNESCO 1977).

5 The Belgrade Charter, together with draft versions and an account of the developments at the Belgrade workshop which yielded the document, are included in Fensham (1976).

6 This working document is Chapter 3 of UNESCO (1977), *Education and the Challenge of Environmental Problems*.

7 These principles draw on and are consistent with those developed by the BA/BEd Review Committee of the School of Education at Deakin University on May 18, 1983.

References

Bennett, D. (1977), 'The evaluation of environmental education learning', in United Nations Educational, Scientific and Cultural Organization, *Trends in Environmental Education*, UNESCO, Paris.

Bernstein, B. (1971), 'On the classification and framing of educational knowledge', in M. F. D. Young (ed.), *Knowledge and Control: New Directions for the Sociology of Education*, Collier Macmillan, London.

Brown, L. (1981), Action research: The teacher as learner, Unpublished paper, Education Department of Victoria, Melbourne.

Buzzati-Traverso, A. (1977), 'Some thoughts on the philosophy of environmental education', in United Nations Educational, Scientific and Cultural Organization, *Trends in Environmental Education*, UNESCO, Paris.

Carr, W. (1983), 'Educational research as science', in A. Pitman et al., EED302 *Educational Enquiry: Approaches to Research*, Deakin University, Vic.

Carr, W., & Kemmis, S. (1983), *Becoming Critical: Knowing Through Action Research* (ECT432/732 *Action Research in Curriculum*), Deakin University, Vic.

Carson, R. (1962), *Silent Spring*, Houghton Mifflin, Boston, Mass.

Commoner, B. (1971), *The Closing Circle: Nature, Man, and Technology*, Knopf, New York.

Elliott, A., & Adelman, C. (1976), 'Innovation at the classroom level', in The Open University, *Innovation, the School and the Teacher (1)* (E203 *Curriculum Design and Development*), Units 27 & 28, The Open University, Milton Keynes.

Environmental Education Project (1980–1981), *Environmental Education: A Sourcebook for Primary Education, Environmental Education: A Sourcebook for Secondary Education, Exploring Outdoors, Streets, Walmit Divided*, Curriculum Development Centre, Canberrra.

Eulefeld, G. (1979), 'The UNESCO-UNEP programme in environmental education', *European Journal of Science Education* 1(1),113–18.

Fensham, P. (1976), *A Report on the Belgrade Workshop on Environmental Education*, Curriculum Development Centre, Canberra.

Fensham, P. (1978), 'Stockholm to Tbilisi – the evolution of environmental education', *Prospects* 8(4), 446–55.

Fensham, P. (1984), Tape-recorded interview conducted on 1 May at Monash University.

Fuller, W. (ed.) (1971), *The Social Impact of Modern Biology*, Routledge & Kegan Paul, London.

Hancock, J. (1971), 'Environmental problems and the reunification of the scientific community', in W. Fuller (ed.), *The Social Impact of Modern Biology*, Routledge & Kegan Paul, London.

Henry, J. A. (1980), 'Inquiry teaching: A failed innovation?', An address to the Catholic Teachers' Association of Victoria, Melbourne.

Henry, J. A. (1981a), Group-based action research at Deakin: Some background and an introduction, Paper presented at the 11th Annual Meeting of the South Pacific Association for Teacher Education, Adelaide, July.

Henry, J. A. (1981b), Teachers as researchers: A redefinition of the theory/practice gap, Paper presented at the Annual Conference of the Australian Association for Research in Education, Adelaide, November.

Henry, J. A. et al. (1981), The professional development of teachers through involvement in action research projects, Paper presented at the 11th Annual Meeting of the South Pacific Association for Teacher Education, Adelaide, July.

Holdren, J. P., & Ehrlich, P. R. (eds) (1971), Introduction in *Global Ecology: Readings Toward A Rational Strategy For Man*, Harcourt Brace Jovanovich, New York.

Hungerford, H. (1983), The challenges of K–12 environmental education, Paper presented at the First National Congress for Environmental Education Futures: Policies and Practices, University of Vermont, Burlington, Vt, August.

Hungerford, H., & Volk, T. (1984), 'The challenges of K–12 environmental education,' in A. B. Sacks (ed.), *Monographs in Environmental Education and Environmental Studies*, vol. 1, SMEAC Information Reference Center, Ohio State University, Columbus, OH.

Hungerford, H., Peyton, R., & Wilke, R. (1981), 'Goals for curriculum development in environmental education', *Journal of Environmental Education* 13(1), 24–7.

Hungerford, H., Peyton, R., & Wilke, R. (1983), 'Yes, environmental education does have definition and structure', *Journal of Environmental Education* 14(3),1–2.

Iozzi, L. A. (1984), Science-technology-society: Dealing with conflict issues in elementary and secondary schools, Paper presented at the 13th Annual Conference of the North American Association for Environmental Education, Chateau Lake Louise, Alberta, October.

Jeske, W. E. (1978), 'Toward an action plan: A report on the intergovernmental conferences on environmental education', United States Department of Health, Education and Welfare, Washington, DC.

Kemmis, S. (1982), 'Action research', in T. Husen & T. H. Postlethwaite (eds), *International Encyclopaedia of Education: Research and Studies*, Pergamon, Oxford.

Kemmis, S. (1987), 'Program evaluation in distance teaching: Against the technologisation of reason', in ECS803 *Curriculum Evaluation and Case Study*, Deakin University, Vic.

Kemmis, S., & Robottom, I. (1981), 'Principles of procedure in curriculum evaluation', *Journal of Curriculum Studies* **13**(2), 151–5.

Liebmann, H. (1973), *Ein Planet wird unbewohnbar*, Piper, Munich.

Lucas, A. M. (1979), *Environment and Environmental Education: Conceptual Issues and Curriculum Interpretations*, Australia International Press and Publications, Kew, Vic.

Malcolm, C. (1984), 'Science education: Where to?', *Lab Talk* **28**(1), 8–11.

Malthus, T. (1972) 'A summary view of the principle of population (an excerpt)', in C. J. Troost & H. Altman (eds), *Environmental Education: A Sourcebook*, Wiley, New York.

Meadows, D. H., Meadows, D. L., Randers J., & Behrens, W. W. III (1972), *The Limits to Growth*, Universe Books, New York.

Popkewitz, T. (1983), *Change and Stability in Schooling: The Dual Quality of Educational Reform* (ESA841 *Theory and Practice in Educational Administration*), Deakin University, Vic.

Robottom, I. M. (1983), *Environmental Education Project Evaluation Report*, Curriculum Development Centre, Canberra/Deakin University, Vic.

Robottom, I. M. (1984), 'Why not "education for the environment"?', *Australian Journal of Environmental Education* **1**(1), 11–13.

Robottom, I. M. (1985), 'Evaluation in environmental education: Time for a change in perspective?', *The Journal of Environmental Education* **17**(1), 31–6.

Robottom, I. M. (1987), 'The dual challenge for professional development in environmental education' in *Environmental Education—Past, Present and Future: Proceedings of a Seminar and Workshops*, Australian Government Publishing Service, Canberra.

Sacks, A. B. (1984), Preface, in A. B. Sacks (ed.), *Monographs in Environmental Education and Environmental Studies* vol. 1, SMEAC Information Reference Center, Ohio State University, Columbus, OH.

Skilbeck, M. (1981), Foreword, in Environmental Education Project, *Environmental Education: A Sourcebook for Primary Education*, Curriculum Development Centre, Canberra.

Smolicz, J. (1974), 'Fragmentation in science and education: An analysis of the community structure of science', in S. Murray-Smith (ed.), *Melbourne Studies in Education 1974*, Melbourne University Press, Melbourne.

Stapp, W. B. (1978), 'Elements of a national strategy for environmental education', in W. B. Stapp (ed.), *From Ought to Action in Environmental Education* (A Report of the National Leadership Conference on Environmental Education), SMEAC Information Reference Center, Ohio State University, Columbus, OH.

Stapp, W. B. (1982), General evolution of educational thought, Unpublished paper, University of Michigan, Ann Arbor, Mich.

Tuttle, F. (1976), Foreword, in S. A. Allman, O. W. Kopp & D. L. Zufelt, *Environmental Education: Guidelines and Activities for Teachers*, Merrill, Columbus, OH.

United Nations Educational, Scientific and Cultural Organization (1977), *Education and the Challenge of Environmental Problems* (UNESCO/UNVED 4), UNESCO, Paris.

United Nations Educational, Scientific and Cultural Organization (1977), *International Programme in Environmental Education* (UNESCO/ENVED 5), UNESCO, Paris.

United Nations Educational, Scientific and Cultural Organization (1977), *Trends in Environmental Education*, UNESCO, Paris.

United Nations Educational, Scientific and Cultural Organization (1980), *Environmental Education in the Light of the Tbilisi Conference*, UNESCO, Paris.

Volk, T., Hungerford, H., & Tomera, A. (1983), A national survey of curriculum needs as perceived by professional environmental educators, Unpublished paper, Southern Illinois University, Carbondale, Ill.

Wilke, R., & Leatherman, J. (1982), Conclusions and generalisations drawn from *Research in Environmental Education 1971–1980* regarding teacher training preservice, teacher training inservice, community resource use and field trips, Unpublished paper, University of Wisconsin, Stevens Point, Wis.

Wilke, R., Peyton, R., and Hungerford, H. (1980), *Strategies for the Training of Teachers in Environmental Education*, UNESCO, Paris

Womersley, J., & Stokes, D. (1981), 'Environmental education: A conceptual framework', in Environmental Education Project, *Environmental Education: A Sourcebook for Primary Education*, Curriculum Development Centre, Canberra.

Annotated bibliography

Kuhn, T. S. *The Structure of Scientific Revolutions*. 2nd edn. University of Chicago Press, Chicago, 1970.

The key proposition advanced in this book is that science is socially constructed. Kuhn adopts a 'sociology of scientific knowledge' perspective, replacing the (hitherto) apparent unassailability of the objective logic of science with a social and historical perspective which permits a critical examination of how science is developed and conducted.

If Kuhn's thesis about the social structure of science is correct, then the scientific community is espousing the qualities of objectivity, rationality and truth while at the same time adhering to a particular set of values embedded in the scientific paradigm of the day. Through the medium of knowledge generated under the auspices of scientific objectivity, rationality and truth, science imposes a set of social values (those held by the supporter of the dominant paradigm) on the wider society.

Kuhn's pioneering work on the sociology of scientific knowledge enables the development of a different perspective of the role of science in environmental education. Rather than being seen as the best (and perhaps only) source of a single, positive and certain solution to each environmental problem, science can be viewed as merely another form of consciousness contributing to the explication of the contested, value-laden decision-making processes involved in all environmental issues. Further, Kuhn's' work encourages the questioning of the proper role *in education* of applied science approaches to problem solving in environmental education.

Popkewitz, T. S., Tabachnick, B. R., & Wehlage, G. *The Myth of Educational Reform: A Study of School Responses to a Program of Change*. University of Wisconsin Press, Madison, Wis., 1982.

As the title suggests, this book concerns itself with responses of schools to planned change and as such is relevant to a consideration of environmental education as an attempt at educational reform.

The main focus of the book is the inextricable relationship between the educational values and practices of schooling (and of attempts to change education) on the one hand, and the social, historical and political views of the wider society on the other. The authors claim that:

> Schooling is . . . a socially constructed endeavor characterized by specific patterns of work, conceptions of knowledge, and occupational ideologies. Since social conditions and constructs reflect social values concerning principles of authority, legitimacy, and control, the nature of these values cannot be taken for granted and must also be scrutinized. Nor can we leave unquestioned how reform programs change or sustain the particular social patterns and values found in schools. (p. 8)

This perspective of the social structure of schooling is consistent with Kuhn's view of the social structure of science in that both point to the (often unacknowledged) social structure of professional work. A recognition of the social structure of professional work is important in the development of a rationale for a critical form of participant inquiry that engages (in the authors' terms) the 'dispositional quality of schooling' and is particularly relevant in the case of environmental education.

United Nations Economic, Scientific and Cultural Organization. *Environmental Education in the Light of the Tbilisi Conference.* UNESCO, Paris, 1980.

This book is an interpretation of the important intergovernmental conference held at Tbilisi, USSR, in 1977. It goes beyond mere description of the proceedings of the conference and a listing of its recommendations to provide a coherent, developed view of environmental education which expands many of the key issues raised at Tbilisi and sets the conference's extensive recommendations in context.

The conference was organised as part of the UNESCO International Environmental Education Programme, and this book was published three years later by the same organisation. Its value lies in the fact that it is both a manageable account written in accessible language and a successful attempt to break the shackles of conventional technocratic intepretations of environmental education. For example, it distinguishes between science education and environmental education in a way that not only points to the limitations of applied science approaches, but also warns of the more general disempowering influence of 'recourse to technocracy'.

> . . . scientific education itself has its limitations, since all segmentation of knowledge is valid only within strictly determined fields. Ill-equipped to recognize these and confronted by a real world that never calls for the application of partial knowledge, individuals are not always able to find solutions to problems and tend to take refuge in the irrational. The problems of the environment are indeed complex ones. They involve numerous parameters and interrelations. Lacking the necessary knowledge and approaches, individuals admit defeat and hand the problems over to the specialist. It is in terms such as these that recourse to technocracy is frequently justified. The result is the abandonment of any attempt to involve ordinary people, who come to be regarded as mere operators or consumers. (p. 26)

Thus this book, in addition to achieving the aim of recording a landmark event in environmental education, adopts a critical stance and raises the important issue of the need for reform in environmental education.

Contributors

GIOVANNA DI CHIRO is a lecturer in the Curriculum Studies Centre of the School of Education, Deakin University, Victoria. Before entering the field of education, she worked as a marine biologist in the Puget Sound, Washington, and was a part-time seaweed farmer. More recently she has been involved in the development and teaching of environmental education at primary, secondary and tertiary levels. Before joining Deakin University in 1986, she worked on developing action research approaches in environmental education improvement at the University of Michigan, Ann Arbor, where she received her Master of Science degree in environmental education.

At Deakin University Giovanna's work has revolved around action research in curriculum, curriculum evaluation, case study methods and environmental and science education courses at the pre-service and post-graduate levels. She was a founder of Deakin University's School of Education Women's Forum and is a member of the editorial collective of a Geelong feminist newsletter. She participated in the planning and organisation of the Australian Association for Environmental Education Conference at Lorne in 1986. Her current research interests include feminist praxis and environmental education, gender relations in education and schooling, action research as political practice and the role of education in social transformation.

NOEL GOUGH is a senior lecturer in the Department of Curriculum and Teaching at Victoria College, Clayton, Victoria. He taught biology, science and media studies in Victorian high schools before moving to the institution now known as Victoria College in 1972. Since then he has developed and taught a number of teacher education programs, including a post-graduate course in curriculum administration and pre-service courses in curriculum design and futures studies. He also teaches Master of Education courses in curriculum study at the University of Melbourne and is Australian editor of the *Journal of Curriculum Studies*.

Noel contributed to the Curriculum Development Centre's Environmental Education Project and has been a member of Council of the Environment Teachers Association (Victoria). He is convener of the Environmental Education Curriculum Committee of the Ministry of Education, Victoria, an examiner of environmental science (a subject in Victoria's Higher School Certificate) and a member of the Australian Academy of Science Environmental Studies Working Group.

ANNETTE GREENALL is the Director of Environmental Education in the Commonwealth Department of the Arts, Sport, the Environment, Tourism and Territories, Canberra, a position she has held since 1983. She taught science, biology and geography in Victorian secondary schools before joining the Curriculum Development Centre, Canberra, where she was Coordinator of Environmental Education from 1974 to 1981.

Annette has published books, articles and kits on environmental education including, in 1981, her University of Melbourne Master of Education thesis, *Environmental Education in Australia: Phenomenon of the Seventies*. She has been a consultant to the United Nations Environment Programme, has represented Australia at several international environmental education meetings and was President of the Australian Association for Environmental Education from 1984 to 1986. She is a member of the Australian Academy of Science Environmental Studies Working Group and the Steering Committee for the Royal Australian Institute of Architects Built Environment Education Project.

IAN ROBOTTOM is a senior lecturer in the Curriculum Studies Centre of the School of Education at Deakin University, Victoria. He taught science and biology in secondary schools in Melbourne before joining the State College of Victoria at Geelong as a lecturer in science method and environmental studies. His Master of Education thesis at the University of Melbourne was on innovation in the science curriculum. He joined Deakin University in 1977 and completed his PhD on environmental education as educational reform.

Ian was an evaluator of the Curriculum Development Centre's Environmental Education Project and is a member of Council of the Australian Association for Environmental Education and editor of the *Australian Journal of Environmental Education*.

BOB STEVENSON is engaged in research at the National Center on Effective Secondary Schools, School of Education, University of Wisconsin – Madison, Wisconsin. He is an expatriate Australian, having taught in secondary schools in New South Wales and worked in the Curriculum Branch of the Queensland Department of Education. In the latter position he was State Liaison Officer for the Curriculum Development Centre's Environmental Education Project and was commissioned by the Curriculum Development Centre Project to write a paper titled 'Developing a school policy on environmental education'.

Bob's recent published work includes a critique of the epistemological and pedagogical assumptions underlying environmental education curriculum materials and several papers analysing research on school change. His current research involves the teaching of higher order thinking and student engagement in academic work, the latter for his PhD thesis.

Acknowledgments

Figure 1 in A. Greenall, 'A political history of environmental education in Australia: Snakes and ladders', reproduced by permission of the CDC and A. E. Greenall from Curriculum Development Centre Environmental Education Committee, Interim Report, 1975, p. 16, as cited in A. E. Greenall, *Environmental Education in Australia: Phenomenon of the Seventies* (A Case Study in National Curriculum Development), Occasional Paper no. 7, CDC, Canberra, 1981, p. 145.

Figure 2 in A. Greenall, 'A political history of environmental education in Australia: Snakes and ladders', reproduced by permission of A. E. Greenall.

Extracts from *Environmental Education in the Light of the Tbilisi Conference* © UNESCO 1980, and from a UNESCO document ref. ED-77/CONF.203/COL.3: *Education and the Challenge of Environmental Problems*, 1977, reproduced by permission of UNESCO.

Extract from Women and Geography Study Group of the Institute of British Geographers, *Geography and Gender: An Introduction to Feminist Geography*, reproduced by permission of Century Hutchinson Publishing Group.

'I am a dangerous woman' by Joan Cavanagh, in Cambridge Women's Peace Collective, *My Country is the Whole World: An Anthology of Women's Work on Peace and War*, and extracts from L. Stanley & S. Wise, *Breaking Out: Feminist Consciousness and Feminist Research*, reproduced by permission of Associated Book Publishers (UK).

Extracts from P. Strange, *It'll Make a Man of You: A Feminist View of the Arms Race*, reproduced by permission of Mushroom Books.

Figure 1 in N. Gough, 'Learning with environments: Towards an ecological paradigm for education', reproduced by permission of *Curriculum Perspectives*.

Extracts from P. Fensham, *A Report on the Belgrade Workshop on Environmental Education*, reproduced by permission of the Curriculum Development Centre, 1976.

Extracts from H. Hungerford, 'The challenges of K–12 environmental education', reproduced by permission of the author.

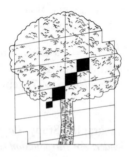